The Country Year

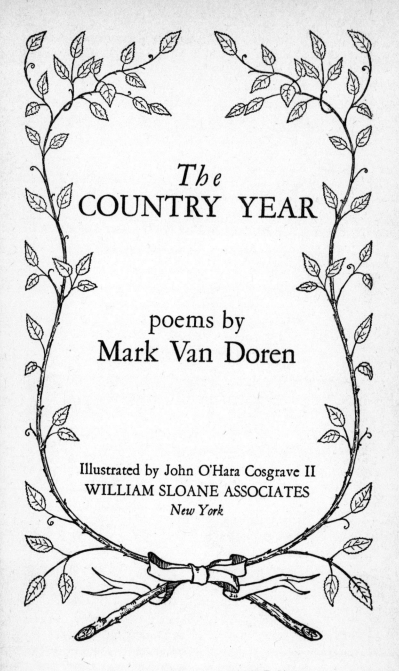

The
COUNTRY YEAR

poems by
Mark Van Doren

Illustrated by John O'Hara Cosgrave II
WILLIAM SLOANE ASSOCIATES
New York

The author wishes to thank *Harper's Magazine* for permission to reprint "Camp Night" and "Sleep, Sleep"; *The Atlantic Monthly* for "The Chickadee"; and Henry Holt and Company for the poems reprinted from *Collected Poems*. "A Hundred Minnows" (page 42) is reprinted by permission of *The New Yorker*, Copyright 1945, The F-R. Publishing Corporation.

DEC 12 1946

112097

To

JOHN VAN DOREN

Contents

Spring Thunder 1

Immortal 2

Former Barn Lot 3

Too Early Spring 4

Good Night 5

Wind in the Grass 6

Alfalfa Coming 6

Alteration 7

Dispossessed 8

Fallen Barn 9

Pigeon 10

Beastless Farm 11

Relief from Spring 12

Crow Madness 12

Tree Dwellers 13

The Bird Watcher 14

Rain Crow 14

Midwife Cat 15

Contemptuous 16

Barricade 16

History 17

Deduction 17

Driver Lost 18

Berkshire Express 19

Water Wheel to Mend 21

June 22   23

Song   23

Turkey Buzzards   24

In Time of Drouth   25

The Runaways   26

Grass   28

Noblesse   29

Night Lilac   30

Ferns   31

Land Tide   32

Company Gone   33

Sleep, Sleep   34

The Tuning Fork   35

Walking the Boundaries   36

Circumferences   37

Down World   38

Gift of Kindling   39

The Pond Ages   41

Camp Night   42

A Hundred Minnows   42

Pond in Wartime   43

Time and Water   44

Eighth Day   45

After Dry Weather   46

At Last Inclement Weather   47

Travelling Storm   48

Rain All Day   49

Contest   50
Invincible   51
Wet Year   52
Waterfall Sound   53

7 P.M.   55
Fall   56
Inference   56
Crow   57
Premonition   58
Coming Home Carelessly   58
One Fall   59
The Translation   60
September Highway   61
Trimming Time   62
Third Growth   63
Apple Hell   64
Apple Limbs   64
Spread, Spread   65
Poorhouse Dream   66
Highway Ghost   68
Big Mare   69
Afterward   70
Bailey's Hands   71
Bailey's Widow   72
Lady of Where She Lived   73

ix

She Is the Youngest   74
The Chickadee   75

December 22   77
Winter Fields   78
Remembered Farm   79
Mountain House: December   80
The Other House   81
Looking Yonder   82
River Snow   83
Deserted Hollow   84
The News of Snow   85
Epistle to Town: February   86
Woodpile   87
Old Orchard   88
Dark Barn   89
The Pulse   90
This Amber Sunstream   91
On Such a Day as This One   92
Midland   93

A Winter Diary   95

Preface

Living in the country, like living in New York, is living in a myth. I am devoted to both experiences, and enjoy them in whatever periods circumstance makes necessary or possible. But the present collection of poems, written over twenty-five years, confines itself to the older ritual. If no poem in it was conceived in the expectation of being thus collected, all of them now seem to me consistent in their desire to record the peculiar excitement of being where animals, people, and objects pass regularly under the review of those four kings, the seasons.

The seasons group the poems, though often in but an approximate or general fashion. The seasons as such are not my subject. Perhaps not even the country is, for I suspect that all poems, mine or others, in so far as they try to be true, are concerned with a single subject the name of which will never be found. But I have observed that a number of my own poems stick close to country matters. And here those are, in the faith that where they come from is a familiar place. I hope, however, that they will succeed in stating the strangeness I discover there along with the familiarity. Living anywhere is living in a myth. It is both simple and not simple, both routine and irregular, both reassuring and—it may be—terrifying.

My landscapes are Illinois and Connecticut. I have not troubled to keep these apart, nor in the arrangement of the poems have I paid any attention to the order in which they were written. Eight of them are new. The accent, I should add, is not always as autobiographical as it may seem. *A Winter Diary*, the last and longest poem in the book, is exactly what it professes to be: a history of one family's country winter. But many another poem here is intent upon things which millions before me, I am certain, have seen or heard or understood.

M.V.D

New York
1946

Spring Thunder

Listen. The wind is still,
And far away in the night—
See! The uplands fill
With a running light.

Open the doors. It is warm;
And where the sky was clear—
Look! The head of a storm
That marches here!

Come under the trembling hedge—
Fast, although you fumble.
There! Did you hear the edge
Of winter crumble?

Immortal

The last thin acre of stalks that stood
    Was never the end of the wheat.
Always something fled to the wood,
    As if the field had feet.

In front of the sickle something rose:
    Mouse, or weasel, or hare;
We struck and struck, but our worst blows
    Dangled in the air.

Nothing could touch the little soul
    Of the grain. It ran to cover,
And nobody knew in what warm hole
    It slept till the winter was over,

And early seeds lay cold in the ground.
    Then, but nobody saw,
It burrowed back with a sun-white sound,
    And awoke the thaw.

Former Barn Lot

Once there was a fence here,
  And the grass came and tried,
Leaning from the pasture,
  To get inside.

But colt feet trampled it,
  Turning it brown;
Until the farmer moved
  And the fence fell down.

Then any bird saw,
  Under the wire,
Grass nibbling inward
  Like green fire.

Too Early Spring

The wind is mighty in the maple tops,
And the long grass is double.
The house leans that way too; but it stops,
Like a bubble,

Swaying softly. And there you walk
With the morning under your skirt.
When blossoms blow from a tender stalk,
Do they hurt?

Does it hurt, now, as you reach the gap,
And part of you whips the wire?
Go back in and straighten your lap
By the fire.

Good Night

This moonlight lies
Like a lovely death
On the darkening eyes,
On the yielded breath

Of the earth, that turns
So quietly now;
Letting its burns
Be soothed somehow

In the widening bloom,
In the tender blight.
It has entered our room.
We sleep tonight.

Wind in the Grass

Are you so weary? Come to the window;
Lean, and look at this.
Something swift runs under the grass
With a little hiss

Now you see it rippling off,
Reckless, under the fence.
Are you so tired? Unfasten your mind
And follow it hence.

Alfalfa Coming

Rain last night has left the field
    Bare as though a goblin kept it;
Inch by inch the fellow kneeled
    And picked it clean; and his wife swept it.

Tomorrow morning when I pass
    A million particles will shine,
As if the sky had been of glass
    And had fallen, shattered fine.

But on the third day will appear,
    Green between me and the sun,
Behind each clod a mouse's ear.
    I will go softly, lest they run.

Alteration

I did not ask to have the shed
   Pulled down, although it leaned so sickly.
But, now the proper word is said,
   Let it come quickly.

Bring rope and pulley, axe and bar,
   And while you hammer I will pry.
Shingles can be sent as far
   As feathers fly.

Naked beams can tumble faster
   Than cobwebs in a sudden gust;
Floors can stand on end; and plaster
   Soon is dust.

I did not think this valley view
   Deserved that any roof should fall.
But, now the word is said by you,
   I want it all.

Dispossessed

No hand had come there since the room was closed
To all but what could live with sifting chaff,
And dust, and pale grey webs. Mine at the latch
Startled the silence; and the wind I brought
Whirled powdery dust against the darkened panes.
No other sound; and so I went to work,
Making a room to put a table in
And sit where none could see me all day long.
No sound. I pulled a length of lining-board
Loose from the timbers, and a spider ran.
Another, and a wasp was at his hole,
Lifting an angry wing. I said of them:
They saw me, but with eyes no man can feel;
I still shall be alone; and laughed and pulled—
And did not laugh again; or go again.
For all I know the dust is quieter now
Than ever it was; with only the bright-black eyes
Of motionless mice on a beam to say if it is.

Fallen Barn

The sun came white upon these shingles once,
And a few rotted edges let it in.
But the hay held it, as it held the rain
That dripped on other days and slowly dried.
No sky ever could pierce to where the stalls
Gathered familiar gloom. Their corners filled
Each year with heavier cobwebs, and the dust
Mingled with many odors never dead.
But yesterday a neighbor hitched four teams
In turn to all the uprights; and they fell.
The sun has followed through, and soon the rain
Will soak the oldest timbers into sod.
Here in the weeds a manger plank was thrown.
You see it, bitten thin. The horse is gone
That found it every evening with his nose
And smoothed it, long ago. Nothing remains
Of what it was that made these beams a barn.

9

Pigeon

This bird is used to sitting on bright ledges
And looking into darkness. Through the square
High window in the barn the mow is black
To one here by the fence. But there he sits
And treads the sun-warm sill, turning his breast
Toward all the musty corners deep within.
They flash no colors on him, though the sky
Is playing bronze and green upon his back.
Gravely he disappears, and spiders now
Must hurry from the rafter where his beak
Searches the seed. The afternoon is slow
Till he returns, complacent on the ledge,
And spreads a breast of copper. But the sun
Is nothing to a pigeon. On the ground
A grain of corn is yellower than gold.
He circles down and takes it, leisurely.

Beastless Farm

The paths again are solid green
    That used to whiten in a drouth,
Whirling dust into the clean
    Heifer's nose and horse's mouth.

Stanchion-leathers crack and fall;
    Water runs, and is not heard.
No sudden thunder from a stall
    Stops a mouse, or starts a bird.

Fences might as well come down;
    Lanes are only ghosts of lanes:
Staring hither with a frown
    At smoke of rumps, at mist of manes.

Relief from Spring

Pastures trickle and shine in this new sun;
Hill roads gurgle; and hocks of shaggy horses
Drip with the melting mud. The winter is over,
And all of the world you know is water again.
But have no fear for the grass. It will not drown.
Yesterday noon I waded the upper meadow
And saw, in the farthest field, a lonely crow.
Where crows will walk it has to be dryer soon.
Crows have taken the very top of the world.
They caw, and the wind is warmer, and there is a rustle
Already of weeds to please their horny feet.
Listen now. The grasses are listening too.

Crow Madness

There is no mandrake here to cry
As fingers rip it from the ground;
But any morning I can lie
And listen to the other sound

Of darkness tearing clear across
And fragments falling with a shriek
On lonely meadows, where they toss
And rise again with angry beak

That plucks at day and offers war
Against the green, against the blue;
Till night, returning, reaches for
All things that lost her as she flew.

Tree Dwellers

Ants file past
To the end of the last
Thin twig, and finding
An ultimate, vast
Green meadow, graze;
While back in the maze
Of the body are winding
Worms in the dark,
That never this bark
Shall open to show
One small bird binding
Straws in a row,
And treading them, so.

The Bird Watcher

He is not lifted by their flight
Across the circle of his sight;
He is cold, and he is slow
Beside the least of them that go
And never heed the silent face.
But there is something that can race
With any wing, and no one see.
A piece of him is flying free
Beyond the further forest now;
And all the beating hearts allow
A path among them to be cut
By these wings that cannot shut;
By this beak that cannot learn
Of any season to return.

Rain Crow

I walked the woods to find it, but no bird
That fled me as I wandered was the one.
There, always in the distance, poured the slow,
Pure, melancholy song, and though I turned
I never could come nearer; till the woods
Grew silent a long time, and I went on
And entered a cool chamber that the trees
Hung dark and close above. It was a room
With a clean floor, and the walls tapered up
Until I thought I stood in an old bell,
Grey ribbed and mossy green, that had not rung
For centuries, and would not ring again.
Then suddenly it sounded. A deep note
From some high hidden corner floated down,
Falling upon my ears; and soon the place
Flowed full of the sad music I had sought.
I waited, with my eyes upon the ground.
I would not lift them up to see a bird.

Midwife Cat

Beyond the fence she hesitates,
    And drops a paw, and tries the dust.
It is a clearing, but she waits
    No longer minute than she must.

Though a dozen foes may dart
    From out the grass, she crouches by;
Then runs to where the silos start
    To heave their shadows far and high.

Here she folds herself and sleeps;
    But in a moment she has put
The dream aside; and now she creeps
    Across the open, foot by foot,

Till at the threshold of a shed
    She smells the water and the corn
Where a sow is on her bed
    And little pigs are being born.

Silently she leaps, and walks
    All night upon a narrow rafter;
Whence at intervals she talks
    Wise to them she watches after.

Contemptuous

Lying along the window sill,
With a low fire to feed his purrs,
He sees a misty meadow fill
With fly-light, that only blurs

And disappears the more he turns;
But comes again and dances down
The rainy slope to where it burns
The tops of trees. He seems to frown

And gaze away at rug and chair,
And settle further from the glass.
Not for him the dripping air,
Not for him the weeping grass.

Barricade

Come to the other hole, and fit your tin,
And start your spike;
And if you hear the rat within,
Strike!

Rats can gnaw, but suddenly a nail
Can eat an inch.
Let him see our teeth, and quail
And flinch.

Now he scampers—pound more loudly yet
To kill my fear.
The feet are what I must forget.
Hear?

History

I crossed the swinging bridge, and there
   The little town I came to see
Was ashes. In the April air
   Ruined rafters poked at me.

I ran, imploring why and when,
   But though I searched on every side
The little town was bare of men;
   The very voice of it had died.

Only past a pile of stone
   Was any sound. I crept, afraid.
There upon the grass alone
   Nell, the shepherd bitch, was laid

And seven puppies pulled at her
   That never saw the little town,
Or the angry wagoner
   Who whipped his horses up and down.

Deduction

So smooth a field,
With the hummocks mown;
Moss peeled
From trunk and stone;

A stunted blade
Withdrawing under
A wall, afraid
Of the herd's thunder:

Only sheep
Could have kept it so,
With nibble and leap,
And lambs in tow.

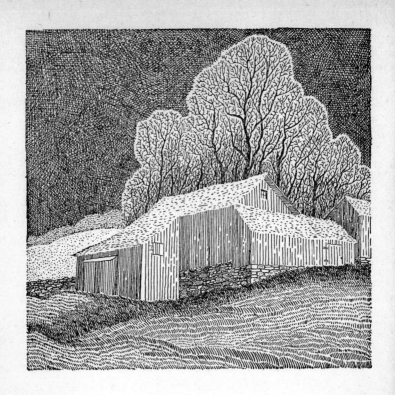

Driver Lost

Roads are flowing everywhere
   In the night, beneath the moon.
But one of them the homing mare
   Is certain of; and soon

The barn will be in plainest sight,
   Grey beyond the grove.
To her the misty way is bright,
   As if another drove.

She points an ear at every turn
   Before a hoof arrives.
What hand is here from which to learn?
   Who is it sits and drives?

Berkshire Express

Starting gardens, whichway from the tracks,
From the May train, look shivery this morning.
Yet there they spread, complacent to the cool,
And hug what they have buried: happy graves
To the hot germs within that swell in rows,
That steam in secret: embryo July.

A little further and the engine climbs,
And all outdoors is tilted. We between
Go barren as the first explorers went,
Sowing but echoes. Sound is all that sleeps
Up the cleft world; and sleeps forever, folded
In a brown skin that June turns into green.

But then no more than green. The buried rock
Hides nothing but itself where under moss
It centuries. What foison could be here?
Nothing but surface sundered into cubes
And rondures. Stubborn death it is, and beautiful,
Balancing those yielders by the sea.

Water Wheel to Mend

There have been times I thought these paddles moved
To music, not to water. Should that hush,
And cataracts descend here with no song,
The axle would not answer with its groan;
The great spokes that swung in solemn circle
Would ponderously wait upon new tunes.
But water still is noisy in the sluice,
And the splashed wheel is motionless. The stream
Foams out below with even a louder voice,
Calling upon the mighty arms to go.
They cannot go; the axle, old and deaf,
Is unaware this spring of water sounding.

Up and around as far as her old eyes,
Opening young and warm, can see they swing;
And swing; and swallows
Take them a little farther, daring the wind.
They are off there now, in the quiet,
And here she sits indifferent, playing blind.
One smile she has for all of the rounded day;
One face she turns, and says that this is the time
For sitting and letting the mind go run with the hours.
There is nothing to fear, she says;
In a field so wide and white no body could die.
She smiles and fingers flowers and, lifting her head,
Listens softly; and swallows
Take her a little farther, daring the sun.

Song

To be at all, you birdlings,
On this or any bough,
Were cause enough for singing
Summer is now.

It is. But very being,
In so much cold and dark,
Is reason for your music;
That time will mark;

Saying it is for summer
As something more. As this:
When all of space, enormous,
And feathers kiss.

23

Turkey Buzzards

Silently, every hour, a pair would rise
And float, without an effort, clear of the trees:
Float in a perfect curve, then tilt and drop;
Or tilt again and spiral toward the sun.
They might have been a dream the timber dreamed;
But could have been a conscious thought, that cut
The warm blue world in segments. For the sky,
Unmeasured, was too much that afternoon.
It lay too heavy on us. Happy trees,
If they could so divide it, wing and wing!

24

In Time of Drouth

The sun this morning is of no avail,
Shining upon a land that cannot cast
One sparkle back. The walls are dead with dust;
The maples do not lift a single leaf;
And all of the way to the village, down our slope,
The meadows have forgotten being green.
Yet look to the left a little. There is brightness.
There, in the angle of two ancient fences,
Dark tall cedars spread their pleasant boughs
Over a few white gravestones that the sun
Now catches full. You see them flash and smile.
Only the dead this morning are not old.

The Runaways

Upon a summer Sunday: sweet the sound
Of noon's high warmness flowing to the ground;

Upon a summer Sunday: wide the song
Of strengthless wings that bore the sky along;

Upon a summer Sunday: strange the power,
Inaudible, that opened every flower;

On Sunday, in the summer, through the white
Mid-world they wandered, meditating flight.

With every boundary melted, still they ran,
Still looked for where the end of earth began;

Still truant; but, dissolving far ahead,
The edge of day as effortlessly fled,

As innocently distanced all they were
Of quick-eared dog and fat philosopher.

On Sunday, in the summer, down a field,
Leader and led, alternately they wheeled

Till the great grass possessed them, and the sky
No longer was a map to measure by;

Till round and round they floated, lost and small,
Like butterflies that afterward will fall

But now between the great sky and the ground,
Sun-tethered, dance all morning meadow-bound.

Upon a summer Sunday, when the light
Of perfect noon was everywhere and white—

Pure death of place and color—then the pair
Grew sudden-silent, hungry for home's air;

Paused, turned; remembered shadows in a yard;
And had again their own high wall and hard.

Grass

Poppies are burning; daisies dip their faces;
The gentle ageratum at my side
Offers a pale blue cheek to the afternoon.
Something has brought the swallows whence they hid;
They tumble up and dizzy the warm day,
Speeding against the calm or dropping straight:
Dropping to cut and float. Along the walk
A black hose runs, and ends in a tall spray;
Catbirds hop to the bath, and flirt and shine.
I look, but do not see these things; or care
When a brown, erring rabbit bounces in,
Fears the immaculate garden, and is gone.
Further across the way there quietly feed
A few round sheep in a shade. And out of sight
Momently there is a pattering among branches,
And ripened apples thud upon the ground.
I look and look, but do not see these things.
My mind is lost in the river of bright green
That, smoothly out from between those highest elms,
Issues under the sun. It does not pause,
But dreaming spreads and flows. So I am taken
Beyond all flutter of birds, all cry of flowers,
All nibble and leap and fall, to lie in grass.

Noblesse

The stubble is an upstart thing,
    A summer's growth, that as we walk
Turns—the envious underling—
    And stabs us with its stalk.

Weeds, arriving everywhere,
    Are insolent as soon as come.
They shout upon the morning air
    Until the flowers are dumb.

But in this corner, past the gate,
    Safe from where the horses turned
I used to lie till it was late;
    And here it was I learned

How bluegrass is the gentlest born
    Of all the gentle things that stand,
Holding, without a spear or thorn,
    Hereditary land.

Night Lilac

Lilac alone,
Standing so quiet, so dim, outside
Till the door light died
On cricket and stone,

Do you sleep at last?
Or beyond this night that has taken my yard
Do you stare more hard,
In a night more vast,

At the great white things
That move the outermost world: the whale,
The stallion, the pale
High planet with rings,

The raven, the bull,
And the midnight mountain that never is black?
Lilac, come back!
My lawn is too full

Of the dark; and the fine
Impalpable shadows will never be still.
Return as you will,
Dim lilac, and shine.

Ferns

When the red road decayed
Their roots were made.
Where the old serpent lies,
Along the gulley and up the wood,
With brambles starting from his eyes,
They thrust and stood.
Only as far on either hand
As ruin could go
They laced the land;
Rising as now they rise to blow
Their branchèd breath
On the body of death;
Keeping it cold,
Keeping it green
Within this mold
No man has seen.
So the old serpent lies
With ripened berries in his eyes.

Land Tide

The moon is in flood;
All things are going:
Grass uprooted
And fences flowing

Over the roads
And the meadows east
To the black immovable
Woods at least.

But the pump, there,
Knows how to resist.
The moon comes on;
It never will twist

And topple and go
As the current is laid;
With its rock root,
And pillar of shade.

Company Gone

Mountains, stand again,
And flowery hay, put up your head.
They are gone, the ten
Men
That flattened you with nothing said.

Lilac, come alive,
And coreopsis, turn about.
They are gone, the five
Wives
You always shun because they shout.

Rambler, tie your shoe,
And Emily Gray, go on along.
We are here, the two
True
Mouths that move but to your song.

Sleep, Sleep

Sleep, sleep, slug in the sun,
Be limp forever, like warm grass.
Be lost to shape, be legs and arms,
Be body separate, be sweet soul
That melts and spreads like innocent **spring**
When time undoes it. Be green song
That sighs unto itself and dozes;
Dries, and into summer brown
Relaxes. So be young and dead,
Beloved, be as nothing there,
There in the sun while I keep watch,
There with the grass while I remem**ber**.
Sleep, sleep, beloved of worlds
That will be jealous, will awake you.
Sleep, until they stand and ask
Who this was by you all the while.
Forget me now, though, sleep and sleep,
Slug of my heart, O nothing of mine.

The Tuning Fork

One dead tree
With arms upswung,
Silver cold,
Is the forest's tongue.

In the middle of the morning,
When the crows cry,
This oldest oak—
None saw it die—

Shrills with its far
Thin finger ends;
Till the body listens
And a scream descends

And the alleys open,
Making room
For another death
In a dateless gloom.

35

Walking the Boundaries

We of this place who prowl its rectangles
Of pine, with their dominant oaks, their maples
That plume an old mountain, are less all alone
Than we think. Four on one side of a wall;

Or a wire, sometimes, that pierces the trunks
Where invisible staples stick in the heart;
Or nothing whatever up ancient stretches;
Only a line the memory draws:

Four of this place, presuming its limits,
Prowl in a thicker silence for something
That watches, something that hears; that presses
Hard on the wall, the wire, yet bends

No boundary: living and dead, our neighbors,
Nodding and prowling too, their confines
Never confused: identical ends
With these, the sunless, the solitary.

Circumferences

Swallows' wings
In the day are swift,
And the hawk's drop,
And the lark's lift,

And mice's feet
That run to cover,
And the sidewise look
Of a jealous lover.

Light is racing
Round the seas;
And thought can distance
All of these.

But faster yet—
And what beyond?—
Is the curving edge
Of a quiet pond,

Or any arc
As soon as drawn,
That seems to sleep,
And plunges on.

Down World

No animal so flattens to the ground,
Hiding and sliding, as clear water will:
Its belly nowhere different from the back
Of the sloped earth it hugs, head downward still.

Spineless, it takes all shapes except the serpent's
With his neck hooped, when anger in him stares.
Water is faceless; for it leaves its features,
Spendthrift, on the very stone it wears.

Men cannot pick it up, the stubborn creeper.
Jointless it lies, head downward, sucking sand.
Yet they will try; there is no older plaything
Than gravity delayed, than banking land,

Than the filled gulch, than levelness extended
Till a wave backward laps, till boats can ride.
So the dam holds. But deep at its foundation
Heave the sunk shoulders, not to be denied.

The sodden eyelids, weary of themselves,
Dream of the crack to come, the pouring through;
Then the parched bed, abrasive, and the close
Going once again down world and true.

Gift of Kindling

Between the pond and brook
A table of fern land,
A sweet, surprising lawn
Where two trees stand:

Wolf maples, that were cause,
Deep shaders, that could bring
This miracle to pass,
This delicate wood ring

Whose center now is hearth;
We laid those lichened stones;
And many a summer night
We picnic on the bones

Of that old buck, the silence,
Or of that fawn, the fear;
We burn whatever creature
Was immemorial here.

Yet with the glade's forgiveness.
For not a time has been
But dry limbs, dropping,
Have said, let smoke begin.

The Pond Ages

Where the brook turns a tile brings down four inches,
Under the poplar roots, and splashes it here
At the tip end; then it broadens, and then it quiets,
And pours out over the stone dam by that building.

Since the first gush descended, and the hardpan
Held it, and the new clay banks were soaked,
Earth has found out about our store of water,
Still as it is, and deckled its trim shape.

The fringes time has planted run uneven:
Sawgrass headlands, bulrush promontories
Where the frogs leap, and undermirror ferns
That tadpoles tickle, growing to be great.

And so the bottom, layered with slow silt,
Softens, and a green cloud daily gathers
Till the frost comes to clear it; but brings leaves
And sinks them: food for worms, and, God knows whence,

For the three trout a bird one noon was proof of.
See? The dead limb? We looked, and a swart kingfisher
Flashed, doubling our knowledge. Yes, we have counted
Three that can show for sticks, then off like shadows.

So the pond ages, letting its edges in
And filling with things that thicken it, that slip
Like earth's own fingers, busily over each other,
Greedily stitching solid what was free.

Camp Night

A little water will put out the fire.
But wait. A little wood will keep it breathing.
It is a heart we started with ten sticks
That now are nothing, like a hundred others
Shrunk to this hectic person whose last life
Would drain the whole cool forest if it could.
Another handful, then, though it is late.
So much in little, such a hungry principle:
We are not lightly to extinguish that.
Quiet a little longer, while it hisses
And settles, keeping secret the sore word
That soon enough its embers will forget.
Our own existence, partly. A wild piece
Of me and you we presently must drown.

A Hundred Minnows

A hundred minnows, little-finger length,
Own the slim pond. In sets they make
Maneuver: all one way
Change-minded, yet of one mind where clear water
Clouds with their speed an instant;
All one speed, one purpose, as they veer
And suddenly close-circle; and some leap—
There! at an unseen fly,
There! at nothing at all.
Brown minnows, darkening daily
Since the thin time, the spring,
Since nothingness gave birth to such small bones,
Beat the soft water, fill
The wet world; as one,
Occupy movement, owning all August,
Proud minnows.

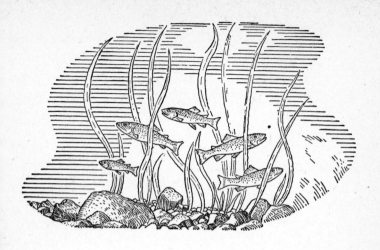

Pond in Wartime

So far from sirens and the fear of wings
That fold not, so content with the one foe
Whose hunger, not whose anger, flexes plumes
And hovers: how explain it, the cold luck
That keeps five trout I know forever gliding,
Ever in weedy corners hunched and hiding?

I see them there as though the summer still
Kept green for me and warmed the vacant fields
They knew not, spreading sideward from their pool.
Nor do I have it now, the crossing land,
Nor can I bend, arriving, and count backs
To the slim fifth, the sluggard, the late born

Who dreaded me too little, and I laughed.
He would not know it now if I should name him
Lazy; no one crosses the brown stretch
And shadows winter water. Even if there
I shouted, they are dozing, the deep five:
Safer than luck interprets, and more live.

Time and Water

The humped back of the beaver, and the four
Curved teeth that bring the poplar splashing down—
There in the lake it lies, and the silver branches
Turn, in the day, in the night, to a watery brown—
The upthrust and pond-dividing whiskers
Say that the world is wet, and seasons drown.

Swimming in darkness, nearing his willow dam,
Pausing before he climbs to the dripping sticks,
He is eternally far from hills and deserts,
Roads, and the odorous barns, and the drying ricks;
The beaver is only credulous of meadows
A rising river enters and moistly licks.

Diving in darkness, down to the lily roots,
Turning and paddling off and rising slow,
The beaver descends again and finds his burrow,
Rises again and is home, and he says: I know.
Water is endless, time is an undulation,
Water is all there is, and seasons flow.

Eighth Day

Water goes all ways; ships go one,
And now we can see what was never there before:
The low grey line where the ocean will be done;
Though yet there is nothing, no green shore;

Nothing but a faint thing that might have been fog,
No painted houses, and no small sheep
Scattered down broken cliffs, underneath a dog
Who growls at the water; but he will never leap.

Water goes all ways; fields keep fast.
Let me lean and look, then, if only at a cloud.
Ninety miles in lies the meadow where I last
Walked beneath a bird, and it was bright, and it was loud.

After Dry Weather

If the people under that portico
Are happy, and point at the pattering drops;
If barehead boys are parading below
Musical eaves of tall house tops;

If you lean out of the window here,
Contented so with the pavement's shine,
And laugh as the covers of cabs appear
With passengers in them dressed to dine;

If all of the stones that we can see
Are licking their lips, that waited so long,
A meadow I know to the north of me
By a hundred miles has caught the song.

I am certain the clover has lifted its head
For dark, intemperate draughts of rain.
Once even I thought I had heard the tread
Of a plunging horse with a sodden mane.

At Last Inclement Weather

At last inclement weather.
After a month of death—
Of holding it and staring—
Day grins; blows out its breath;

Grimaces; and, deep-growling,
Furies the bated air;
Of which the lack-love atoms
Had fainted pair by pair.

Now in the wind's excitement
They dance a tumbled round:
Their first and only madness,
Their single rage of sound.

Invisible the clashing;
Unheard the little cries;
Save that in us they echo;
Our particles uprise—

Dimensionless, dark pieces,
Yet are they fiery strong—
And sting us with their whirling,
And lift us high and long;

And threaten us with flying
Like cannon balls apart;
Save that the skin is thinner,
And tougher next to the heart.

Travelling Storm

The sky above us here is open again.
The sun comes hotter, and the shingles steam.
The trees are done with dripping, and the hens
Bustle among bright pools to pick and drink.
But east and south are black with the speeding storm.
That thunder, low and far, remembering nothing,
Gathers a new world under it and growls,
Worries, strikes, and is gone. Children at windows
Cry at the rain, it pours so heavily down,
Drifting across the yard till the sheds are grey.
A county farther on, the wind is all:
A swift dark wind that turns the maples pale,
Ruffles the hay, and spreads the swallows' wings.
Horses, suddenly restless, are unhitched,
And men, with glances upward, hurry in;
Their overalls blow full and cool; they shout;
Soon they will lie in barns and laugh at the lightning.
Another county yet, and the sky is still;
The air is fainting; women sit with fans
And wonder when a rain will come that way.

Rain All Day

The sky is laid as low again
As once it was when fearful men
Heard the hoarse chime
Of moving time.

Over me now unmuffled feet
Trample the blue, and flatten the sweet
Flowers of day
That sang him away.

As up they sang the distance grew
Between our faces and these two
Merciless heels
My forehead feels.

Space is fallen, time is found,
And we are nothing but the ground
On which he walks,
Mashing the stalks.

Contest

The east wind I worked in,
And endless black rain—
Working with a wet axe
As long as there was wood—
The rain, the wind, and I
Argued which should die.

The chopper never looked up,
Behind him or around;
Only at the wet log
His blade fell and warmed;
Hoping heat would spread
Until the dark was dead.

The wind never looked away,
But, always coming on,
Drove the rainy knife edge
Deeper in and in.
It was the day that died
With blue in its side.

Invincible

Rain, that wets powder,
Slows axles,
Blinds bombers,
Gurgles in grass roots too, and clover;
Steadies the knees
Of flowers, of trees
That soon will surround
A burst battleground.

Rain, that delays
Far meetings,
Fierce onsets,
Thickens the old hide, doubles the armor
Of earth, that will bleed
No more than it need
When man the newcomer
Seizes his summer.

Rain all the while
Stores noiseless
Provisions;
Tangles the meadows, jungles the woodlots;
Mixes a meal
Of rust for steel;
Is quartermaster
Against disaster.

Wet Year

Six of the other kind were one too few
If this, the dripping seventh, is alike
Complained of. Numbers have no magic in them,
Maiden, if you do not take this mold,
These swollen doors for benison; black days
For blessing. They were asked for, and are given.

The foolish grasses, rivaling the forest:
See how they overreach themselves, and fall
In a green swale that dew will drown tomorrow.
Look. The glade side of every sunless rock
Is heavy with small mosses, smooth or curled;
And some of them are rusting into seed.

The meadow there was sun enough to sickle—
That was before the flood—is high again
As colt's knees. Walkers in it make a music,
Heel and toe, more heady than dark ale
To an old ear remembering last summer;
Or any of the six, the sunburned years.

Not grateful when no trout dies in the brook?
You never see them, even; mud comes down,
Yes, daily. But the level of soaked earth
Sinks daily, nightly; for the sponge is filling.
An old foot loves it, under. Which I know
Is nonsense to the April in your veins.

Waterfall Sound

In the middle of the wood it starts,
Then over the wall and the meadow
And into our ears all day. But it departs,
Sometimes, like a shadow.

There is an instant when it grows
Too weak to climb a solid fence,
And creeps to find a crack. But the wind blows,
Scattering it hence

In whimpering fragments like the leaves
That every autumn drives before.
Then rain again in the hills, and the brook receives
It home with a roar.

7 P. M.

Slow twilight bird,
Suspended, as you sail, along the nearer edge
Of nightfall and the beechwood, are you heard
In places past my ears? Are you a wedge,

Slow tapered wing,
Driving into the outer walls of time?
Eternity is not so strange a thing,
At evening, when the towers that were to climb,

Slow searching beak,
Lie level with your progress in the soft
Dark-feathered dusk, and there are known to speak
Gentle, wild voices from the dark aloft.

Fall

Winter and spring and summer are this or that:
A white old man, a girl, a drowsing tree.
The fall is a covered bridge that crosses the river
Down from my father's house. The foam and the rocks
Grow suddenly to a grey there, as the sky
Returns one day to roof the valley in.
The bridge's darkened mouth, so cool all summer,
Gathers descending leaves; already warm there,
The shadows settle to sleep, and a yellow cart,
Flickering through the leaf-shower down the highway,
Comes on with noiseless wheels and disappears.

Inference

Who made the evening made the fear
Of horse and bird and snake and deer,
Of all that do not learn they live
Till light itself, grown fugitive,
Goes breathing by; but turns about,
And the black pouncer puts it out.
Then bird and horse and deer and snake
Go posting home, before they break
The line that leads them; and their eyes
Hold all the day that slowly dies.

Crow

A hundred autumns he has wheeled
Above this solitary field.
Here he circled after corn
Before the oldest man was born.
When the oldest man is dead
He will be unsurfeited.
See him crouch upon a limb
With his banquet under him.
Hear the echo of his caw
Give the skirting forest law.
Down he drops, and struts among
The rows of supper, tassel-hung.
Not a grain is left behind
That his polished beak can find.
He is full; he rises slow
To watch the evening come and go.
From the barren branch, his rest,
All is open to the west;
And the light along his wing
Is a sleek and oily thing.
Past an island floats the gaze
Of this ancientest of days.
Green and orange and purple dye
Is reflected in his eye.
There is an elm tree in the wood
Where his dwelling place has stood
All the hundred of his years.
There he sails and disappears.

Premonition

It was September, and the weeds were mowed
For the last time along the narrow road.
Sunlight speckled down, as leaves would fall,
Shortly, upon the gravel; and by the wall
Chipmunks quietly ran that soon would sound
More loudly on the green and yellow ground.
A woodchuck crossed beyond me as I went,
So slowly that he seemed indifferent;
As if he slept already out of sight,
Deep in a burrow, with the meadows white.
I soberly advanced, and all the way
Was proof that nothing now could ever stay
Of the soft summer. Even when I stood
At last upon the border of the wood,
And the bright Hollow lay a mile below,
The light dazzled, and I thought of snow.

Coming Home Carelessly

Coming home carelessly,
Nine thoughts away,
The tenth took it in—So!
The dog days are over.

Sultriness never
Survived such a green
Last evening as lay,
Mint strip on the hills,

And sliced the long summer,
And sheared the heat's end.
But I came alone; so
Eleven is yours.

One Fall

Time grew so thin
That it could hang
Between these hills,
Where nothing sang

Save the silence.
All those weeks
Are now as one;
And it speaks—

Sharply now—
Of a suspended
Year that died
Before it ended;

Leaving only
A blue shell,
That turned to brown,
And never fell.

The Translation

Ant and shrew
And marmot, going
Safely there,
The time of mowing

Comes tomorrow.
Meadow lark
And banded snake,
Then the dark

Sky will fall:
What is green
Above you now
No more be seen.

What is single
Will divide.
And as you run
The other side

Of all the world
Will drop its blue
As if it looked
For none but you.

Toad and cricket,
Worm and mouse,
You will find
Another house

That not a hand
Was there to build.
My own sky
Has never spilled,

Right and left,
And shown a new one.
Night and day
Mine is the true one.

Would it were not,
And could lie
Thus to the sickle
As I die.

September Highway

"Why do you go so fast tonight,
In the endless dark, in the blowing rain?"
"One of these maples spat three bright
Red leaves in front of us, and the stain

"Is deepening there, though no one sees:
Blood on the roadway trickling down.
Summer is wounded high in the trees,
And red is black, and green is brown.

"Yesterday noon our lawn was bare.
So would I climb and find it still.
I am trying to beat the wind up there
That wants it lonely at the kill."

Trimming Time

With clippers, bush hooks, and bent-handled scythes,
And six-foot sickles that a tractor pulls,
We persecute small trees. A hot hay time
Anticipated this, the August hour
When cold dew on the walls invites the upstart
Brush, the fringe of would-be cherry forest
Falling now with summer, willow shoots
That only will be sticks beneath the snow,
Laid there with starting maples and the nipped
Young master oaks we missed another year.
We persecute these infants of a wood
That never will be. Worshipers of shade,
Of great trunks up the mountain where no man
Could meadow, here we hold our open own,
Here hack and slaughter. Not a head must wave,
Not anything shall stand above these stones
Domestic, these diagonal old rows
The sun long since accepted; these clear fields,
Wedging high wilderness that we may be.

Third Growth

The little pine grove, trimmed of its ground branches,
Lets the eye through, a thread among those needles
That sew a green cloud fast to fern and rock.
In their own shade the stems, so black and small,
Are pillars of weak steel; yet nerved enough,
And tempered, to attach for soft eternity
Feathers to earth, wind music to the swell
Of soundless, of grim granite; which the drop
Of other needles, browning, will spread over,
As the grove grows, with carpet for fox feet,
With compost for silence. So the trunks,
Increasing, will be columns that hold up
A weightless, waving mountain; and no man
Will speak of stitches then. This is the time
To see it, to send vision dipping through,
And then downhill by meadows to the Hollow's
Bottom where the bone-white steeple stands.
This is the century for that. Dead villages
Glisten. And the pine begins again.

Apple Hell

Apples, bright on the leafless bough,
In the high noon sun, with the sky above you,
Time will turn. For the white sky falls
And long, red shadows soon will shove you

Eastward, downward, into the room
Where the moon hangs low like a smoking lamp;
Walls lean in; and the studded ceiling
Shines no more; and the bins grow damp.

Apples, yellow on the naked limb,
Although you burn till the air be gold,
Time is tarnish. Skies are falling,
Noon is dead, and the day grows old.

Apple Limbs

Lay them as neatly
Away as the wind
   Lays the soft grasses
   Through which it passes.

They waited all summer,
Just as they fell:
   On gnarl and prong;
   And the time was long.

But yesterday's hatchet
Straightened their knees.
   Now nothing will cumber
   Them in their slumber.

Spread, Spread

Spread, spread, November rain;
Sleep-bringing river, widen so
That every meadow takes the stain
Of rising death's first overflow.

Instruct the trees that are adorned
Too bravely now, and drown their blood.
Leave not a sunwise slope unwarned
Against the white, the final flood.

Invisibly the banks of time
Give way; the unseen river reaches.
The mist of change begins to climb
And slide along the grassy beaches:

Sliding until no further drop
Of dryness lives in any vein;
When even change will, flowing, stop,
And stumps no more remember rain.

Poorhouse Dream

Death is a tall horse
With large white feet,
Coming on a slow walk
Down the long street,

Nudging with a soft nose,
Opening the gate.
Up you must climb then,
Lest you be late.

Starting on a slow walk
And never looking round,
He moves; and the great feet
Never make a sound.

Soon it is a road
With the houses far between,
And when a farm is there at last
Children come and lean,

Shouting over fences;
But not as if they knew.
And not a word arrives
Of what they say to you.

On beneath a bright hill
Is water in a trough.
But he is never thirsty,
And you are looking off,

Thinking of the afternoon,
Thinking of the night.
But all the sky is green there,
And all the hours are white.

He will never halt again,
And you will not descend.
You will be content there
Without any end.

Highway Ghost

The gravelly road is gone.
Old people, whirled behind a windy wheel,
Huddle their coats about them and remember
How they went proudly once;

How the eight ringing feet
Flung gritty pebbles into the grass,
And how the four high iron tires
Sang in the sand.

Old men, silently borne
Where now the way goes black and wide
And smoothly like a river into the wood,
Old men, saying nothing,

See a white horse come curving,
Swinging an empty buggy round the hill.
The white feet fall without a noise, approaching,
And thin wheels lightly follow.

Spokes flicker by,
And grey heads, nodding at each other, turn
To see between the curtains what is there.
Nothing at all is there.

The gravelly road is gone,
And dim eyes, drawn around a bend forever,
Have in them only history, and the fall
Of a slow shadow.

Big Mare

The grass is deep in the field, and her four legs
Sink out of sight. She plunges lazily on
To a fresh circle, whence she lifts her head
And looks across the fences to the barn.
No voice from there, no swing of any door.
She lowers her nose to the ground; but suddenly shifts,
Looks up again; and stares into the quiet.
Yesterday, and as long as she remembers,
At this good hour there sounded a shrill cry—
"Here Chunk! Here Chunk! Here Chunk!"—and two
    thin arms
Were waved from a dark opening in the wall.
Now nothing; so she feeds until the sun
Comes cooler over the meadow, and starts home.
Her feet trample on clover, and her breast
Moves with superfluous might against the weeds.
She ploughs across the creek and through the gap;
Is halfway up the hillside; still no shout;
No corn upon an aged, trembling hand.
She hesitates, as if the barn were gone;
Had never been just here; and gazes long
At the half-opened door; then stumbles through.
Some stranger has thrown nubbins in the box;
Her salt is there; the timothy is down.
She munches, while no words are in her nostrils;
No feet in boots too big for them clump by.
The weak old man who never failed has failed.
Yet foolish whisperings, not of the hay, are heard;
Spidery pads of fingers now caress her,
Swiftly over a shoulder, down a flank,
Smoothing, smoothing her mane till evening is night.
Does a plain mare remember? And how long?
Tomorrow will come a slap and a careless whistle.
Tomorrow will come a boy. Is she to forget?

69

Afterward

The stalls were empty in the shed;
    Nothing grazed beyond the gate.
But there was straw to make a bed,
    And the four bridles dangled straight.

We heard the water running cold,
    As she had left it, round the crocks.
Linen lay for us to fold,
    And there was pepper in the box.

The very trap that he had set
    To catch a mole that loved the lawn
Hung above the passage yet;
    Another mole was boring on.

The wounded deer still fled the dog
    Within the gold and walnut frame;
The Fishermen Among the Fog,
    And The Young Mother, were the same.

We laughed to see a boot behind
    The stove; but then you wept
At your happening to find
    Spectacles where she had slept.

Bailey's Hands

The right one that he gave me—
I could have shut my eyes
And heard all seventy summers
Rasping at their scythes.

The left one that he lifted,
Tightening his hat—
I could have seen the cut groves
Lie fallen, green and flat;

Or seen a row of handles,
Ash-white and knuckle-worn,
Run back as far as boyhood
And the first field of thorn:

The two-edged axe and sickle,
The pick, the bar, the spade,
The adze, and the long shovel—
Their heads in order laid,

Extending many an autumn
And whitening into bone,
As if the past were marching,
Stone after stone.

So by his hands' old hardness,
And the slow way they waved,
I understood the story:
Snath-written, helve-engraved.

Bailey's Widow

Still there, as if the weathered house
Were tomb and low memorial; no shaft,
No sky thing, but a hugger of such earth
As he with horizontal craft
Knew webwise; we remember how he kneeled
And studied every silver herb afield.

Still kitchen table bound, by windows
Wiped to keep the headstones far and clear;
Still huge among her trinkets: catalogues,
Gilt cards, rag balls, and cooking gear,
She sits, the clock a goddess overhead
Less watched than watching, like the distant dead:

An old man under gravel, sidewise
Peering; and she rubs the pane to see.
Yet more that he may feel how still the cats
Prowl round her, blinking up; how three
Small dogs dispute the blessing of her lap;
And how she sometimes nods to him by nap.

Lady of Where She Lived

The round old lady with the little eyes—
Lady of where she lived, of the split shingle
Walls, and the warped door that let four cat feet,
Cat feet in—the white old one, she perished
Even as planned. For where she lived she was lady,
And the lamp knew it that she tilted over:
Tilted, and it poured obedient flame
Due upward till the cupboard papers caught.
There must have been more oil in secret places,
For the first valley warning was the last;
The windows were too bright, then not at all
In the one peak of red, the pyramid
She built, this queer old queen, to shrivel under.
The cat feet, cat feet fled among the highway
Asters, and they never felt again
For the gone door she must have heard them pressing
Till the warp freed them. They are wild now,
As she is, but they were not sacrificed.
She ended it alone. And lives alone
In the one place of which she could be lady,
The wild place of weeds; and of these clockworks,
Melted at the hour, the little minute,
He the lean one left her years ago.

She Is the Youngest

She is the youngest of the wood,
Yet is there many a newer thing.
The hemlock with the ragged hood
Droops in everlasting spring.

Above the snow, or when the leaves
Lie well around her, safe and dead,
Not a wind but lowly weaves
The delicate spine; deflects the head;

Picks up the green and greyish cape
That all but flowed into the earth.
Grave, grave the maiden shape,
Out of love awhile with mirth.

Sad, sad, but it is well:
How she looks upon the ground
Cures the melancholy spell
Of age and coldness all around.

Sad, sad, but what she means
Is that the world is old and strong;
Indulgent still to one that leans
On youthful sorrow overlong.

The Chickadee

The chickadee has three short songs
To love the world with, spring and fall;
And winter,
For he loves it all.

And two of them are cherry sweet,
But one is diligent persimmon;
Children
Love the last, and women.

And it is cheerful at the door,
In snow, when nothing else will sing.
But woodsmen
Hear a different thing.

In ragged pines, in melting March,
Or in September's softer prime,
Two sounds,
Or three, in saddest time:

Most plaintive, as the happy heart
Can be, pretending. So they say,
Those men
Alone, and look away.

December 22

Noon today and the earth swings high—
Swing low, you sun whom once she loved—
Noon, and her body is trying to die;
And horses stop, and men go gloved.

Noon in the north, but never an end—
Look far, you sun whom still she knows—
Try as she may, she cannot bend
Backward enough for the eyes to close.

Stiffly at noon now, under the lids—
Look in, you sun, and remind her now—
She stares once more, though her will forbids;
And mice dream on in the darkened mow.

Winter Fields

Once they were black
And again they were green.
But the sun dropped,
And the wind grew lean,

And the crows dived
So fiercely down
That the grass blanched
In meadow and town;

And barns and fences
And rows of trees
Died to a brown
As brown as these.

Whatever can live
With the sun so low?
That wagoner there
But appears to go.

Soon you will look
And the wheels will stand:
Frozen asleep:
Locked in with the land.

Remembered Farm

There was a line of frosty light
Along each roof and down the road.
All the rest was perfect night;
Not a field or window showed.

In my cool thought no morning came
To sweep the hills, no moon arose
To flood the meadows with its flame
As far as all this valley flows.

Now I am come, the fields are fair.
Yet not the greenest flesh atones
For when the skeleton was bare
And lightning ran along the bones.

Mountain House: December

Anyone on the road below
  Can see it now; the boughs are bare
That hung about it months ago,
  Beautiful, and thick as hair.

It is a white and silent face
  That some will talk of, driving by.
None will turn to reach a place
  So cold and high.

No summer walkers up that way,
  Arriving half in shadow, stand
And wait upon the sign to stay
  From a slow hand.

The house's hands are folded in,
  For warmth; but all the warmth is fled:
It climbed the stairs, and stricken thin
  Died one evening on your bed.

The Other House

The leafless road midwinters by itself,
And the slat gate, wired open, never swings.
Should the loop rust, and weaken in the wind,
Two posts will join that now are separate things;
Forgetful how they guarded the little space
One entering coat could fill, one entering face.

We spoke of strangers happening to pass,
And wondered if such openness were wise.
But the posts know; they have not felt each other
Since the high sun was shaded from their eyes.
We spoke of footprints; but a sparrow's track
Is all that diverges in and circles back.

Even a look from us so distant here,
Even a sigh might leave its line on snow:
Up the still road and in, then round and round;
Then stopping, for we must no further go.
Let the line pause mid-yard; there let it end,
Lest the sad chimneys smile, and smoke pretend.

Looking Yonder

Ice on a hundred highways
Keeps seven cities home;
Yet keeps some there at windows,
Prisoners of room;

Keeps me, as morning glitters,
And the street steams with breath,
As blind to what is round me
As though this were death.

But it is looking yonder,
And what lives thus is warm
With something more than crystals
Comforting its form.

One small slope of mountain
May know when I come over
By how I name the meadows,
The moss ones, the clover;

By how I see through whiteness
To the least rock and mouse
Where ledge runs into woodland,
Opposite that house,

That house with sleepy buildings
Haloing its head;
I count the folded ladders,
The wood in its cold bed,

The kerosene, the hanging
Saws; and even by day
The stall with its hot lantern,
Lengthening wild hay.

River Snow

The flakes are a little thinner where I look,
For I can see a circle of grey shore,
And greyer water, motionless beyond.
But the other shore is gone, and right and left
Earth and sky desert me. Still I stand
And look at the dark circle that is there,
As if I were a man blinded with whiteness,
And one grey spot remained. The flakes descend,
Softly, without a sound that I can tell;
When out of the further white a gull appears,
Crosses the hollow place, and goes again.
There was no flap of wing; no feather fell.
But now I hear him crying, far away,
And think he may be wanting to return.
The flakes descend. And shall I see the bird?
Not one path is open through the snow.

Deserted Hollow

This valley sends another sound
Than was delivered of its rocks
When they were seized and set around
The cloven feet of little flocks.
The sheep were taken long ago,
And fences wait a wilder foe.

There is no hushing of the wind
Between the blows of axes now.
No breathless timber-lengths are pinned
And shingled fast to make a mow.
There is not one expectant eye
Upon the purpose of the sky.

It was a race of silent men
That taught the clouds to hesitate,
If only to upgather then
A blacker heavenful of hate.
Riders up and down divided
Weather since grown single-sided.

Winds that strike upon these stones
Hear not an angry voice among them.
They have smothered their old moans
Against the hairy hands that wrung them.
Boulders, grass, and border-trees
Supinely harken. Fences freeze

And crumble wider every spring;
They will yet be flat again.
There is not a wilful thing
In all this patient mountain-pen.
There is only the dead sound
Of slowly unresisting ground.

The News of Snow

The news of snow full driven at the face,
Or settling, settling, not to be denied,
Comes on and on, as if the world had waited
Only till now to show its other side:
Then all at once, for whispers in the air
Say walls have turned, and white is everywhere.

And it comes on. For not the cold, the blowing,
Not the shy rustle where the leaves were shed,
But always, always the arrival hither
Of what was yonder once, of what was dead:
This is the outer, this the ancient thing
That shrugs and comes, as if a shroud could sing.

As if the ash were all, the hoary cloak
Worlds wear to show that time is done with them;
As if immensity, that murdered earth,
Now cast its mold, its powdery diadem;
So the lost atoms, ending themselves here,
Whisper in white at so much nothing near.

Epistle to Town: February

Go to your table, in the lined room
Outside of which four ashmen used to bark.
Go to your table, to the lettered keys.
Send me words quickly, on small hard feet,
Tapping this snow that is too soft and wide,
Dotting this white that is too everywhere.
The trees stand out of it, and bushes blow
Thinly, as if they meant to creep indoors.
Yet nothing moves; all things are waiting here,
And the sky waits upon a dance of words.
Let them say anything, so they are black,
So they come suddenly on little heels,
Dropping like seed upon this tablecloth.
Say I am a crow, and have a hungry eye,
Fed now too long upon an empty field.
Think of me hovering. Tell me a taxi
Halted just now and let a lady out,
And she went into Number 45.

Woodpile

The high heap that now and then,
When the wind thumps it, settles—
The breathing space decreases for the grass
Beneath it, and the nettles—
Will lie, when April thrashes,
Compacted ashes.

Not here, not like this mountain, tossed
From the saw's teeth all fall;
Not here, but humbly leeward of the house,
And ghostly small.
Nothing, after this winter,
Of sap or splinter.

There will be nothing of the difference,
When grass grows again,
Nothing between the big and little mountains
Save two unfrozen men:
The blood in them still running,
Lukewarm and cunning.

For such as them this pyramid
Must pass, becoming flame—
All but a little powder on the ground there
That no lit match could tame.
Lest their poor lives be finished,
Bulk is diminished:

Shrinking until a room expands
To summer under the snow;
Melting away though earth is solid iron,
And ice-flakes blow.
Perhaps itself should stay.
Yet who can say?

Old Orchard

Hardly a trunk but leans,
Hardly a top but holds
One bony limb, one curving
Tusk: death's head in spring.

And there it thrusts all summer,
And there it waits in snow
For feebleness sufficient:
Snap, and the sudden plunge.

And such we burn, with praises
For purple fire: the fuel
Of kings, we say; forgetting
The king himself is there.

Or pieces of him. Slowly,
Grandly, apple dies.
Cords of him stand barren
Still among the leaves.

Tons of him, as heartwood
Still in sun and wind,
Will heat the bones of better
Choppers scarcely born.

Dark Barn

Windows, dying, left for dust
The wings of flies that spiders trussed
And waiting speared. The door is held
With weeds that not a blade has felled,
With vines that thicken since the last
Inlooker shut the shadows fast.
It is a piece of darkness saved
Against the summer, and the waved
Bright hair of harvest, brought to shear.
Nothing will cut the darkness here,
That grows and fills the rafter spaces,
Hangs, and wraps the rusted traces
And blind bridles on their pegs;
Stares between the stanchion legs;
And is the only thing to know
That running mice bear pretty snow
Upon their bellies, which they hide
For joy beneath them as they glide.

The Pulse

One thing is sure
When most are not:
That there is cold,
That there is hot.

There is no error
In the frost;
With warmth away
No warmth is lost;

Waves are coming
Of a time
That has been written
In slow rhyme:

Hot and cold,
And cold and hot;
All things may fail,
But this one not.

Though hate and love
And mercy cease,
Under the rippling
Vapor fleece

Of earth goes warmth
Pursuing cold;
And neither is young;
And neither is old.

This Amber Sunstream

This amber sunstream, with an hour to live,
Flows carelessly, and does not save itself;
Nor recognizes any entered room—
This room; nor hears the clock upon a shelf,
Declaring the lone hour; for where it goes
All space in a great silence ever flows.

No living man may know it till this hour,
When the clear sunstream, thickening to amber,
Moves like a sea, and the sunk hulls of houses
Let it come slowly through, as divers clamber,
Feeling for gold. So now into this room
Peer the large eyes, unopen to their doom.

Another hour and nothing will be here.
Even upon themselves the eyes will close.
Nor will this bulk, withdrawing, die outdoors
In night, that from another silence flows.
No living man in any western room
But sits at amber sunset round a tomb.

On Such a Day as This One

On such a day as this one, time and sky
Flow round our shoulders mingled past division;
Past asking which, past hearing, for on high
One silence broods: the ultimate elision.

Such a day as this one lifts the seas
And loses them in air—as blue, as thin.
Yet not the seas; there is no current moving;
Not anything translucent, wave or fin.

Such a day as this one is the end;
Or would be if there were no shoulders listening.
Nothing but their question saves the world;
And that high sun, upon the silence glistening.

Midland

Under the great cold lakes, under the midmost
Parallel that Lisbon too lies under—
Vesuvius and Corinth, Ararat,
Peking and Chosen, yellow and blue seas
Enormous, then the redwoods, then high Denver—
Under the wet midnorth, under cool Canada,
Swings my own West, directionless; the temperate,
The tacit, the untold. There was I born,
There fed upon the dish of dreaming land
That feeds upon itself, forever sunk
From the far rim, from crust and outer taste,
Forever lost and pleased, as circling currents
Swim to themselves, renumbering Sargasso
Centuries a wind brings round the world.
There am I still, if no thought can escape
To edges from that soft and moving center,
That home, that floating grave of what would fly
Yet did not: my own boyhood, meditating
Unto no end, eternal where I was.

A Winter Diary

This was not written then, when measuring time
Ran smoothly to unalterable rhyme;
When even song—but still it is unsounded—
Kept the pure tally that has been confounded.
This was not written then, when sudden spring
Not yet had threatened winter, and no thing
Stood colder than the skin of apple trees.
Now every top is bursting into bees;
Now all of them, solidified to light,
Reflect a cloudy fire, as high, as white
As any sky in summer; and at last
Sharp edges of a shadow have been cast.
Thus sudden spring, with sudden summer near,
Has made a certain winter disappear:
The winter of all winters I would keep
Had I the power to put this warmth asleep
And make the world remember what I saw.
But who has power against the seasons' law?
Who lives a winter over, who is proof
Against the rain of months upon his roof?
A certain winter fades that I had thought
Forever in live colors to have caught.
A certain moveless winter more than moves:
Runs backward, and oblivion's great grooves
Lie deeper in the distance, and tomorrow
Nothing will be there save mist and sorrow.
Therefore must I fix it while I may:
Feign records, and upon this single day
Tie months of time together, in pretended
Sequence till they once again are ended.

. . . So it is autumn, when the city reaches,
Pulling us home from mountains and from beaches;
Down the curved roads and from the crescent sands
To oblong streets among divided lands.
Yet not us four. It is the year we stay
And watch the town-returners pour away.
Now the last stragglers of the stream have gone;
Here now we stand upon a thinning lawn—
The shade wind-shattered, and the cut grass sleeping—
Here then we stand and to the country's keeping
Tender four faces. Not a leaf that falls
But flutters through a memory of walls;
Flutters, with more to follow, till they weave
This solitude we shall at last believe.

. . . October sunshine, and a summer's day!
Yet not the heaviness long wont to lay
Slow skies upon our heads and bind us round
With the full growth of a too fruitful ground.
The morning sun was southerly, and noon
Came swiftly, and the day was over soon:
An airy thing time tossed us for our pleasure,
Blue, and wide-blown, and rich with gold leaf-treasure.
The solid green is gone, the trees are fire:
Cool fire, and top-contained, without desire;
Not caring if it lives, for lo, all day
Wind bullied it and bore the sparks away.
October sunshine and red-ember drifts;
So the long burden of a summer lifts.

. . . November rain all night, the last of three
Dark nights and mornings. We have been to see
The brook that piles grey water down the meadows.
Grey water, and there is no sun for shadows;
No wind for bare tree-talk, no thing but spreading
Rain; no thing but rain, wherein the treading

Crow-feet leave thin tracks, and grass is drowned
With a contented and a final sound.
Safely indoors now, with a fire to dry us,
We hear a whole long year go slipping by us—
Backward to die, with nothing left ahead
Save solitude and silence, and a thread
Of days that will conduct us through the cold.
The windowpanes are waterfalls that fold
Small misty visions of our valley's end.
The rain is sewing curtains that will rend
And rise another day; but shut us now
In such a world as mice have up the mow.
Thus do we know ourselves at last alone;
And laugh at both the kittens, who have grown
Till here they lie, prim figures by the fire
Paws folded, aping age and undesire.
The boys would have them up again to play.
But they are sudden-old; it is the day
For dreaming of enclosure, and of being
All of the world time missed as he was fleeing.
They think, the furry fools, to live forever.
So then do we, the curtains lifted never.

. . . It is December, and the setting sun
Drops altogether leftward of the one
Long mountain-back we used to measure by.
The maple limbs swing upward, grey and dry,
And print the lawn, now naked for the snow,
With lines that might be nothing. But we know.
We see them there across the bitten ground,
Dark lace upon the iron, and catch the sound
Of half a world contracting under cold.
Slowly it shrinks, for it is wise and old,
And waits; and in its wisdom will be spared.
So is the frosted garden-plot prepared.
The withered tops, arustle row by row,

Fear nothing still to come; for all must go.
That is their wisdom, as it is the horse's,
Whose coat the wind already reinforces,
There in the blowing paddock past the gate.
The four of us a long day, working late,
Confined her where she grazes, building the fence
She leans on; yet she would not wander hence.
She drops her head and nibbles the brown grass,
Unmindful of a season that will pass;
Long-coated, with a rump the wind can ruffle;
Shoeless, and free; but soon the snow will muffle
All of her four black feet, that study a line
Down to the ponies' corner under the pine.
So have the field mice, folding their startled ears,
Burrowed away from owls and flying fears.
So have the hunters ceased upon the hills;
The last shot echoes and the woodland stills;
And here, along the house, the final flower
Lets fall its rusty petals hour by hour.

. . . So, in December, we ourselves stand ready.
The season we have dared is strong and heady,
But there is many a weapon we can trust.
Five cellar shelves that were but layered dust
Are wiped to kitchen neatness, and confine
Clear jellies that will soothe us when we dine:
Crab-apple, quince, and hardly ripened grape,
With jam from every berry, and the shape
Of cherries showing pressed against the jar;
Whole pears; and where the tall half-gallons are,
Tomatoes with their golden seeds; and blunt
Cucumbers that the early ground-worms hunt.
The highest shelf, beneath the spidery floor,
Holds pumpkins in a row, with squash before:
Dark, horny Hubbards that will slice in half
And come with pools of butter as we laugh,

Remembering the frost that laid the vines
Like blackened string: September's valentines.
Firm corn, and tapering carrots, and the blood
Of beets complete the tally of saved food;
Yet over in a corner, white and square,
Is the big bin with our potato-share.
Then seven barrels of apples standing by.
We brought them down the ladder when a high
Stiff wind was there to whip us, hand and cheek;
And wheeled them to the barn, where many a week
They filled the tightest chamber; but they found
More certain safety here below the ground:
The Baldwins to be eaten, and the Spies;
But Greenings are for betty and for pies.
A dusty cellar window, old as stone,
Lets in grey light, a slowly spreading cone
Sharp-ended here, and shining, at the shelves.
All of the other spaces wrapped themselves
In darkness long ago; and there the wood
Remembers a great sky wherein they stood:
The twenty trees I walked with Louis, marking,
Once in a mist of rain; then axes barking
Through the wet, chilly weeks, with ring of wedges
Under the blows of iron alternate sledges,
Louis's and Laurier's, of equal skill.
These were the two woodchoppers whom the still
Small faces of the boys watched day by day.
They sat among brown leaves, so far away
We barely could hear their shouting as the saw
Paused, and the great trunk trembled, and a raw
Circle of odorous wood gaped suddenly there.
Now maple and oak and cherry, and a rare
Hard chestnut piece, with hickory and birch,
Piled here in shortened lengths, await my search:
Coming with lantern and with leather gloves
To choose what provender the furnace loves.

99

From wall to wall a dozen resting rows:
We shall be warm, whatever winter blows.
So for the range upstairs a mound uprises,
By the back fence, of birch in sapling sizes.
Old Bailey cut them through a lonely fall—
He and his axe together, that was all:
They in a thicket, and the white poles gleaming;
Now a high frozen pile the sun is steaming.
We shall be warm, whatever north wind catches
Any of us outside the rattling latches;
Down the sloped road, or where the yard descends
To the barn's angle with its gusty ends,
Or higher, beyond the garden and the orchard—

We shall not be snow-worried or wind-tortured.
The armor we have sent for has arrived.
The great book spread its pages, and we dived
Like cormorants for prey among the rocks;
And chose, and duly ordered; and the box
Came yesterday. A winter's woolen wraps:
Thick-wristed mittens and two stocking caps;
Three fleece-lined jackets that will turn all weather,
And one cut neat for ladies out of leather;
Red sweaters, nut-brown shirts, and rubber-soled
Great workman's shoes for wading in the cold.
We shall be warm; or we can stamp indoors,
Wool failing, till the supper and the chores.

. . . So quietly it came that we could doubt it.
There was no wind from anywhere to shout it.
Simply it came, the inescapable cold,
Sliding along some world already old
And stretched already there had we perceived it.
Now by this hour the least one has believed it.
Snippy, the lesser kitten, lies entangled
Deep in the fur of Snappy, where a dangled
Feed-sack drapes a box inside the shed.
I found them with the lantern, playing dead:
Those very creatures, Snippy and her brother,
Who in the orange sunset tumbled each other,
Lithe by the steppingstone. Through such a night
How often have they put the frost to flight;
How often, when the blackness made them bolder,
Have they confounded time, that grew no colder.
Yet not this night; they recognize the god,
As in the barn the black mare, left to nod,
Stands in her blanket, dozing. I have come
From tending her, and heard the ominous hum
Of branches that no wind moved overhead;
Only a tightness and a stealth instead.
The stiffened world turns hard upon its axis,
Laboring; but these yellow lamps relax us,
Here in the living room at either end.
She by the south one, I by the north pretend
Forgetfulness of pavements; or remark
How very dead the sky is, and how dark—
In passing, with the air of two that pore
On things familiar, having been before.
It is our way of knowing what is near.
This is the time, this is the holy year
We planned for, casting every cable off.
That was a board-creek; that was the horse's cough;
That was no wind, we say; and looking down,
Smile at the wolf-dog, Sam, who dreams of brown

Clipped fields that he will lope in when he wakes.
He dreams, and draws his ankles up, and slakes
Imaginary thirsts at frozen pools.
He is the wolf-dog, he is the one that fools
Newcomers up the yard; for gentler beast
Prowled never to the pantry for a feast.
He is the boys' companion, who at dusk
Ran rings with them tonight, and worried the husk
Of daylight in his teeth, and stood his hair
Wind-upright. Now he sleeps unthinking there,
Companion of the boys, who long ago
Climbed the dark stairs to bed. So we below
Should come there too, we say; and say it again,
And laugh to hear the clock tick out the ten.
We are not sleepy; this is the holy year.
Let it tick on to midnight, and for cheer
Start coffee in the kitchen, while I spread
Bright jam upon the goodness of cut bread.

. . . We were awakened by a double shout:
"Get up, you lazy people, and look out!"
There was a weight of stillness on my eyes;
But in my ears innumerable sighs
Of snowflakes settling groundward past the glass.
I stood and stared, saying for jest "Alas!
My sight fails, I can see the merest dim
Milk-whiteness!" "We must bring it up to him!"
Cried one; and both were going, when I told them:
"Dress!" So now, as breakfast waits, behold them
Marching through a mist of falling specks.
They stop and raise their faces, and it flecks
Their foreheads till they laugh; then treading on,
Leave tracks across the swiftly thickening lawn.
I let them go this morning for the milk—
The car wheels turning softly in a silk
New coverlet as wide as eyes could see.

The chimney smoke was rising, round and free,
From every ridge of shingles: even there
Where Grandmother waved and pointed at the air.
The wolf-dog running with us need not pause,
Tasting the untamed whiteness; for his jaws
Dipped as he loped along, and fiercely entered
Now the far past wherein his mind was centered.
Back at the barn the Shetland ponies wheeled,
Biting each other's manes, their little field
Grown boundless by some fantasy, and fenceless.
They romped like shaggy dogs, and were as senseless,
Fluttering at the gate, as moths, and small.
They waited for the big one in the stall.
She whinnied as we came, and only stopped
When I rose up the ladder and hay dropped.
She will have finished breakfast in an hour.
So we, and through a sudden whirling shower
Shall bring her to the ponies. Then our talk
Will come once more to sleds, and up the walk
I shall again make promises; and keep them,
Thinking of flakes and how a wind can heap them.
This wind is gentle, and the grey sheet sways.
I am no prophet if it falls and stays.

. . . All yesterday it melted, and at night
Was nothing, and the prophecy was right.
But in a playhouse corner stand the sleds,
Almost as high as the excited heads
Of two that will be on them when the slopes
Glisten once more. And so the boys have hopes
While I have present pleasure; for the ground
Grows musical wherever I am bound.
The mud was gone as quickly as the snow.
An afternoon of thaw, but then a low
Crisp sunset sound of shrinking, and the crack
Of coldness like a panther coming back.
Tonight the snowless evening and the moon
Kept my late feet contented with a tune
More ancient than the meadows, where the stones
Rise ever up: unburiable bones.
The bareness of the world was like a bell
My feet, accustomed, struck; and striking well,
Let the rung sound be mingled with the dry
Primeval winter moonlight flowing by.
Alone outdoors and late, the resonant lawn
Moved with me as I lagged, and moving on
Bore all my senses fieldward to those bones
Of permanence, the unalterable stones.
There is no such intensity of lasting
Anywhere out of meadows, where the fasting
Grasses worship something in December
Older than any moist root can remember;
Older than age, drier than any drouth;
Something not to be praised by word of mouth.
I did not praise them then, nor shall henceforth;
But shall remind me, so, what change is worth:
Timothy round a rock, and daisies hiding
Something that will be there again—abiding
Longer than hope and stronger than old despair;
Something not to be dated under the air.

I looked at stones; and faces looked at me:
Sidewise, always sidewise, past a tree
Or slanting down some corner, or obliquely
Squinting where the moon fell, and as weakly.
I saw them not but knew them: the tired faces
Of those who may not leave their acred places:
Those of a time long gone that never dies.
You know it by the darkness of their eyes,
And by the way they work to comprehend
Who lives here now beyond a century's end.
Who lives and does not labor, and makes light
Of the grim gods that once were day, were night;
That carved a cheek, bent breasts, and knotted hands.
Not one of them withdraws or understands.
Not one of them but looked at me; and I,
Intruder here, seemed helpless to reply.
Not by their older choosing are we here,
Not by their doom made free of gods and fear.
Was then the better time? I said; and thought
How excellently winter moonshine taught
The shapes of winter trees. That maple there,
How shadeless, how upflowing, and how fair!
Even without their leaves the elm limbs drooped;
The alders leaned; and birches interlooped
Their lacy, blackened fingers past the pines.
The great dead chestnut where the loud crow dines
Writhed on, its mighty arms unskilled to fall.
The evergreens were solid over all,
And hickories and tulips, few of limb,
Held what they had straight out for time to trim.
Was then the better world, I wondered—daring
Suddenly now an answer from the staring
People of old days, the accusing faces.
But none of us, tree-watching on these places,
Ever will hear a sentence from the source.
Gone is their blood, and spent their bitter force;

They only live to chafe us down the wind
And leave us ever afterward thin-skinned:
Wondering on them, the only-good,
On whom these lighter feet too long intrude.

. . . We have had company of Friday nights.
We have looked out of windows till the lights
Of cars too long in coming dipped and streamed;
Then ended by the door as time had dreamed.
Two late ones from the city, blinking here
In the warm lamplight, with the kittens near—
These have been shown their room, the spare northeast one;
Have laughed and begged a bite: even the least one,
Even a crust to pay them for the ride.
Already coffee bubbled, fit to glide,
As quickly as cups were ready, from the spout.
Already there were cookies placed about;
And soon the supper entered that would keep us
Longer awake than wise, with talk to steep us
In every winter's moment we had missed.
So we unrolled our pleasures, till the list
Grew endless, and the meaning of it fled.
So, as the boys before us, up to bed.
For all of us a lazy breakfast waited,
With coffee and tobacco, brownly mated,
Warming the day to come. We tilted chairs,
Lit pipes, and fingered forks; till unawares
Time bore us half to noon; and looking out,
We argued what the weather was about.
Some said it would be overcast till night,
Settling themselves forever; but the right
Was mostly with the walkers and the curious.
First then the barn, where the black mare was furious,
Tossing as I excused our long delay.
No answer, but the eyes among the hay
Dived languorously and said I was forgiven.

The cutter by the car could not be driven.
I found it years ago and dragged it here
To a dry floor and braced it; but the clear
Curved figure will be never swift again.
Snow or no snow, it is for living men
Another last reminder of the old
Dim people who are dead. A crimson fold
Of lining flaps and braves the window frost.
But all the rest is poor and language-lost:
No bells to shake, no orders to be going
Down a long hill where only time is snowing—
Flake by flake forgotten, till the white
Far past of it is shadowy with night.
We took the road and turned, and crossed the bridge;
Then, needing not to beg the privilege,
Crossed neighbor Allyn's meadow to his row
Of sandknolls; then, as all the cattle go,
Between the roundest couple home to tea.
So Saturday, and night, when we agree
What games shall silence evening, and what talk
Shall bring the ghost whose breast is brittle chalk.
So Sunday, with a visit to the great
Grandfather pine that guards the burial gate.
Neglected there, the town's first graveyard lies
Where once the Hurlburt roadway took the rise,
Bringing a country mourner up to pray.
But year by year the woodchucks have their way,
And higher mounds are there than used to reckon
The small well-buried length of smith or deacon.
So all the week-end over, and the pair
Departed; and a blizzard in the air.

. . . That second snow fulfilled us while it lasted.
But now for two brown weeks the fields have fasted
Under a windless, under a lukewarm sun.
Christmas Eve and New Year's Day are done,

And here we stand expectant, straining dumbly
Toward a long stretch that will not lie so comely:
Three dark, inclement months before the spring.
Or such the hope; we want no softer thing,
No disappointment deepened day by day.
That second snow, dissolving, drained away
Too much of sudden glory, and too much
Of the towered god whose mantle we must touch.
There was no blizzard in it after all.
Only a thickening sky, so slow to fall
That Monday passed, and Tuesday. Then a hush;
Then a faint flick, as if a fox's brush
Had gained the woods in safety, and the hole;
Then steadily, steadily down the winter stole.
All afternoon it hissed among some clump
Of shrubbery, and deepened round the pump;
All afternoon, till time put out the light.
Then the black rustling through the soundless night:
Dark flake on flake colliding where no gaze
Of beast or person followed. Dim the ways
Of snow in great high darkness; strange the sound
Of whiteness come invisible to ground.
And yet the lamps awhile allowed the glance
Of a stray whirl of moth wings blown to dance,
Confused, beyond the four and twenty panes.
Here once we sat and watched the autumn rains
Stitching a wall of water. Now the snow—
A frailer fall, and gentler—came to sew
New raiment for the sun-accustomed sashes.
The upstairs window that a north wind lashes,
Beating the maple on it gust by gust,
Hung silent, like a picture; but it thrust
Pure light on brilliant branches, layered well
With silver that as slowly rose and fell,
No visible lawn beneath it, and no thing,
Round or above, save blackness in a ring:

A prone, suspended skeleton creeping hither,
All knuckle joints and bare bones twigged together.
Next morning then, with Christmas five days off,
What wonder if we called this well enough?
What wonder if the two boys prematurely
Counted upon continuance, and surely
Bragged of a snowy hill for him, the guest:
The expected boy, of all their friends the best,
Due now from deep Virginia on a night;
Their own, to play a week with out of sight?
So off they hurried, pulling the sleds behind them,
To cross the nearest meadow-stretch and find them
Somewhere a perfect slope that they could pack:
The runners for the hundredth time and back
Deep-sinking through the softness, with dragged feet
To finish a rough design and leave it neat.
I watched them for a little from the road,
Then called, and she came with me to the snowed
White forest edge, and over the wall inspected
The prints of birds; or how a deer directed
Leap after leap to gain his inland thicket.
A pine branch sagged to the earth, but I could flick it,
Filling my neck with flakes as up it reared,
Snow-loosened of its many-pointed beard.
Meanwhile the cry of coasters over the hill,
With moment interruptions, clear and still,
That said the feet were staggering up again.
We came, and Sam the wolf-dog joined them then
In a loud, urgent welcome, bark and word.
For he had crossed the field to make a third,
And close-pursued them, snapping at their feet
Now up the slope, now down; then off to meet
Plump Snappy, most companionable cat,
Who, plowing the snow alone, arrived and sat
Like something stone of Egypt, not for play.
He watched us, two by two, slide swift away,

Then turned his head, encouraging the weak one,
Snippy, the little sister, the grey meek one,
Who half from home had squatted in a track;
And wailed until we saved her, walking back.
That was the day, with four days still to come,
We prophesied long whiteness; hearing the hum
Of trees contracted slowly in no wind;
Or watching the clouds a clear sun dipped and thinned.
That was the night the low moon, all but waned,
Came to me once—upstarting at the strained
Hurt sound of something strangled in the woods—
Came to me at the window, over floods
Of waveless shining silence, and I said:
There is a month of coldness dead ahead.
But Thursday of a sudden thawed it all,
And Friday, like a silly thing of fall,
An innocent late-summer thing, declared
Calm days, with every melting meadow bared.
So when they blew their horn and gained the gate—
Those weary three Virginians—only a late
Cool breath of proper evening blew to greet them.
Sam leapt out ahead of us to meet them.
Then the old rejoicing, four and three;
With talk of the north till bedtime, and the tree
We all must bring tomorrow: a picked pine
To anchor in a room with block and twine.
We found it, best of several by a swamp,
And sawed and bore it hither amid the romp
Of boys and tumbling cats, that on warm haunches
Settled to watch us trim the bristling branches;
Looping the ends with silver-studded cord
And lo, with more than patience could afford
Of cranberries and popcorn needled through:
Now red, now white, now one and one, and two.
From every room, when darkness well was down,
Came packages of mystery, in brown

III

Creased paper if a boy or man were giver;
But if a lady, candlelight would quiver
On multicolored tissue, gold and green.
Then silence, with a glow behind the screen
To point our way to bed, the lamps unlighted.
Then dawn, and stairs acreak, and something sighted
Even beyond the door that we had closed;
Then breakfast, and the mysteries deposed.
No more the ache of waiting; shed the power
Pre-eminent of any future hour.
That was the height; the rest was going down,
With random walks, or driving into town,
Or sitting after sunfall over tea.
We tidied rooms and set the spangled tree
Midway the snowless lawn, and spiked it there—
Popcorn and berries on it, and a square
Of suet tied with string to tempt the flying
Birds. But there were kittens always spying,
Ready to pounce and punish; and at last
A brief wind laid it over like a mast.
The rest was milder pleasure, suiting well
Our seven tongues that had so much to tell.
We talked. And then the final day was come.
Farewell, you three! And if the end was dumb,
Remember this: there was no charm to say
As down the hill your fenders sloped away.
So Christmas Eve and New Year's Day are done;
And still the lukewarm, still the windless sun
Possesses what it watches: hidden here,
A barn and painted house, from which appear
Four little figures scanning a clear sky.
It doubtless will be clouded by and by,
And doubtless yield each one his small desire.
Now only tracks, minute upon the mire.

. . . O welcome night wind, crazily arriving,
You had not warned us till we heard you striving,
Here and at every corner of the house—
Now a great beast and now a nibbling mouse—
Striving in every stature to undo us;
There was no rumor of your marching to us,
No swift annunciation; or eight hands
Loud, loud had hailed you, giving you our lands,
Ourselves, and all this valley to unsettle.
We only lay and heard you; heard the rattle
Of shutters, and caught the groan as you went on
Of nails from weather-boarding all but drawn.
We only lay, pulling the covers higher,
Until at dayrise, grouping about the fire,
We greeted a hundred frost-hills on the panes;
Looked through, and saw the still wind-worried lanes
Thrash heavily; and walking out a little,
Said the snapped, hanging branches were wind-spittle.
Nor was the blowing over; still at twelve
High limbs were double-curving, like a helve,
And through the day, beneath white clouds and round ones,
All was a sea, with us the happy drowned ones—
Drifting among the layers of thin cold,
Self-separated. Some, the slow and old,
Slid lazily, floating beyond a world;
But some were childish-violent, and curled
And slapped our willing foreheads as they raced.
Layer upon clear layer built a waste
Of space for minds to work in, high and low.
Then the loud night that bade the softness go,
With iron for morning ground, and every print
Of dog or man foot stamped as in a mint:
All metal, all eternal, if this cold,
High, many-shelving universe could hold.

It held; and laid a film across the pond;
Laid more, and laying others, brought the fond
Brown wolf-dog there to slide beside the boys—
Bewildered, but enchanted by the noise
Of brittle alder-sticks and clapping hands.
So now the ice in hourly thickened bands
Is pressing tight around us, pond and lawn.
One moment, and the mighty gale was gone,
Far-whistling. Then a silence, and the fall
To nothing. Then the crisp iron over all.

. . . Slap, slap, the sound of car chains going by,
With elsewhere only stillness, under dry
Fantastic heaps of white the wind renews.
It reached us evenly, as snowfalls use;
But there were days of fury when the air,
Whirled white as flour, was powdery everywhere;
Till now the finest grains, like desert sand,
Wait upon eddies they will not withstand.
The snowplows on the highway come and go:
Not vainly, but a devil takes the snow
Some windy times, and then the car lanes fill
Along the leeward side of fence or hill.
The boys are in the snowhouse we had made
Before this blowing weather overlaid
The first wet fall with something crisp as salt.
Four walls we packed without a single fault
Between a pair of solid shutter forms.
A roof, an eastern door away from storms,
Two windows at the ends—a bread knife cut them,
Neatly, but there was then no way to shut them—
A piece of crate for cushion, and a bag:
This is their windy fortress that a flag
Flies every day in front of, and that Sam
Lies guarding, less the dragon than the lamb.
There was a man with anthracite for eyes,

And pennies for his buttons; but he lies,
Forgotten, uncreated, where he fell.
There was a castle wall beyond the well
With store of snowballs piled against a siege,
And apples for the starving, lord or liege;
But now it too is levelled, and delight
Dwells only in this hovel at the right.
Below the sheds and halfway to the wall
Stands a lean icehouse, windowless and tall,
Whose ancient door hung open day by day
Till the last shining cake was stowed away.
When ice was fourteen inches teams were hitched;
Saws buzzed; and like a waterland bewitched
The silver floor divided, line and angle.
Then loaded trucks, with pairs of tongs to dangle,
Teasing the helpful boys until they tried—
Slipped, fell, and were convinced. And so inside
Sleep twice a hundred pieces of the pond,
Preserved against the dog days and beyond.

. . . These are the undistinguishable days.
This is the calm dead center of the maze
Whereinto we have wandered, and in time
Shall wander forth again, and slowly climb
A wall the other side of which is change.
Now everything is like, with nothing strange
To keep our hands aware of what they do.
This is the winter's heart, that must renew
Its steady, steady beating when an embered
Joy is all we have, and thoughts remembered.
Therefore do I listen while I may,
Monotony, to what your whispers say
Of systole, diastole, and the ribbed
Sweet rituals wherein our wills are cribbed.
Therefore shall I count the doings here
Of one full day, and represent the year.
We rise at eight, but I an hour before
Have put the pipeless furnace in a roar;
Descending slow in slippers, robe, and socks
To where, as in some southern ship that rocks,
Dry cargo-wood inhabits all the hold.
Our destination only the days unfold:
Tier on tier down-sloping to warm weather.
But many a hundred chunks lie yet together,
Snug in their odorous rows. So I inspire
Last evening's spent and barely breathing fire;
Pull off my gloves; ascend the under-stair;
And smoke a chilly moment in a chair.
Then up again. But they are coming down,
Each head of hair in tangles at the crown;
And suddenly we smell a breakfast waiting:
Bacon and yellow eggs; or, alternating,
Buckwheat cakes with butter for anointing;
Or third-day porridge, grey and disappointing.
Prepared with steaming water and the comb,
We gather about the range—the morning home

Of kittens, too, and Sam the wolf-dog, stretched
Full length behind it while our plates are fetched.
The Irish hands that laid our dining table
Were up in early darkness, whence a fable
Of ghost or saint, night-walking, has its rise.
We listen, masked amusement in our eyes,
And finishing our fare, proceed to measure
Whether this day is planned for work or pleasure.
There is a woodshed faucet where I fill
Two water pails, and through the winter-still
Bound morning beat the music that she loves:
The restless mare whose foretop, smoothed with gloves,
Will hang with hay-stalk in it while she drinks.
She knows my coming footfall, and she thinks
To speed her slave's arrival with a neigh.
I am too proud to hurry; yet the hay
Seems due her, and the water, none the less.
So up to where last summer's grasses press
Their rustling weight on weight; and casting down
High pitchforkfuls, I stuff the slats with brown,
Stiff breakfast which the clever ponies hear.
I listen to their trotting, small and clear,
Round the curved path to where the western door
Stands open night or day, whatever roar
Of winds or pelt of snow drives ruthless in.
They are from northern islands where the din
Of winter never daunts them. Unconfined,
They wander about the paddock till the mined
Mute hayfall wakes their wisdom. Then they race,
Two blown and hairy creatures, into place.
I leave them there, slow-nibbling, eyes astare,
And go to prod the motor in his lair:
Four thousand pounds inert, and chilled so well
Some mornings I can barely solve the spell.
I have been baffled when a weakened spark
Has failed to fire the monster, and the dark

Webbed shadows of the room have missed his roar.
I have discovered drifts against the door,
And shovelled; I have watched a winter's rains
Turn ice, and been in misery with chains:
Now on, now off, now broken and now mended;
I have as often wished a year were ended.
But now the long thing moves, and backing out
Brings Sam, who disobeys my daily shout
And lopes to where the open meadows tempt him.
I could be angry, but his ears exempt him,
Waiting erect and friendly when I come.
My way was longer round; but now the strum
Of pistons will be answered by his feet,
That guide me to the milkhouse, dark, unneat,
Where the day's pail awaits me. Then the mile
Retravelled, past the cemetery stile
That leads among the six-foot frozen mounds.
There have been mornings when I heard the sounds
Of pick and frozen shovel at a grave;
But mostly snow and timeless silence—save
That cries of farmer children ring in the wood,
Where the white Hollow school long years has stood.
Some of them wave and call my distant name;
Then bells, and marching in to serious game;
While I at my own corner mount the hill
Past Bailey's house, and hers, where now a still
White shaft of smoke that bends above the brook
Declares Grandmother up. A pause; a look;
Good morning to her, cheerful at the door;
Then on to where the barn receives the roar
Of cylinders again until they cease.
Now to the restless mare, whom I release—
High stepping, in perpetual surprise—
To where the ponies shake their shaggy eyes.
All day will they be three beyond a gate,
Ground-musical, and free of their estate;

While we that own them, in and out of doors
Must labor at our self-appointed choŗes.
Now the grey tool house where the chisels hang,
And hammers lie, and saws with sharpened fang
Rest nightly on their nails, invites my skill.
I am no maker, but a floor can fill
With shavings from the least instructed plane.
Or there is wood to split, come snow or rain,
When the black stove grows hungry, and the dry
Deep kitchen box demands a fresh supply.
Ten times the barrow, loaded, piles its pieces
High at the woodshed end, till all the creases
Fold a fair week of darkness, and the dented
Chopping block is with cold wounds contented.
There is one root the garden still can give.
Under the snow, under the stubble, live
Our golden parsnips, planted and forgotten.
Nothing of them is altered or frost-rotten.
The blunt pick thuds in the ground, and up they heave:
A miracle for winter to believe.
I bring them in for dinner on this day;
And while the kettle, boiling their ice away,
Fills half a room with steam I take the road
Once more, to curiosity's abode:
That box where now the mailman will have been.
Arriving slow, I thrust my fingers in;
Draw letters forth, a bundle, or a card;
And out of time abstracted pace the hard
White ground again to where three wait for me.
No ancient courier with a king's decree
Rode ever up a hill and brought so much
As these chilled messages the mind can touch,
Restoring warmth, reviving every word
That yesterday with its own motion stirred.
Meanwhile the boys have had their little school:
Two pupils and a mother, mild of rule,

Who after beds were made and dinner planned,
Called them to where the home-built easels stand
And where the primer waits that one can read.
The younger mind admits a younger need:
Long blocks that tilt together till a boat
Sits sailing; or a castle with a moat;
Or dungeon towers to keep a kitten in—
The almond-eyed four-footed Saracen.
To painting then: tongues out and foreheads glowing,
With bannerets of bright vermilion flowing
Over and up and down; or blues, or blacks,
Full to the very corners past the tacks.
One thing remains: a paragraph to trace
On paper from the blackboard's printed face.
The boy leans long upon the table leaf,
Procrastinating; for the task was brief,
And both of them had still an hour to play.
But there he leans, unwilling, till the day
Brings twelve; and half-past twelve; and brings the white
Sealed letters that are now the noon's delight.
So dinner, and a nap for everyone
Where neither snow may enter nor the sun.
So then the afternoon, that still is short—
Midwinter lags behind the sky's report:
Each day a little longer, but the dark
Comes down before a coaster may remark.
While there is light we seek the genial store,
Off by the covered bridge; or wanting more,
Ride over two east ranges to the town
Of brass that bore the body of John Brown.
Here pavements like a puzzle run and spread;
And here a shop front, gold by gaudy red,
Demands immediate entrance; for a dime
Buys anything, land-born or maritime:
A ball, a wooden car, a masted boat,
An outboard motor that will never float;

A magnet's curve, completed by a bar;
A leaden blue policeman with his star.
So home across the ranges, past the edge
Of evening, till the last high-drifted hedge
Declares the clear necessity of chains.
So out to frosty spokes and windy lanes
Where the snow, blowing, whips the wrist and scatters;
Then upward, while a broken chain-link clatters;
Upward into the barn, the engine dying
Soundless; but the ponies are replying,
Huddled before the big one at the gate.
Scarcely we listen, for we estimate
Two hours this side of supper. Time for tea.
We light the lamps and sip the mystery,
Cup after shadowy cup, with toasted cheese.
There are no country moments like to these;
When afternoon is night, and night belongs
Like a dark heirloom of descended songs
To four that sit in solitude and hear them
Through the fond nothingness that nestles near them.
From the warm circle of the shaded lamp
At last I walk to where the ponies stamp
And the tall guardian mare is loud with thirst.
A boy with lighted lantern sheds the first
Long pair of scantling shadows on the snow;
While I, the water-bearer, dimly go
Through the great backward crescent drawn behind us.
There have been evenings when she would not mind us—
The lurking mare, complacent down the meadow.
But now a clear low whistle cleaves her shadow,
Precipitately arriving. So we lead her,
Plunging, past the corner post; and heed her
Sighing as she nuzzles in the pail.
The lantern from a high and rusty nail
Swings gently, casting circles on the hay.
The kittens somewhere, noiselessly at play,

Keep watch of us, and scan the waiting door.
They love a barn, but love the kitchen more;
And lessons still may linger in each mind
Of the long milkless night they sat confined.
We leave the ponies munching in their room
And blow our lantern black, resolved to come
By starlight home—Orion and the Bears
Low-shining; but aloft upon the stairs,
Bright Castor holding Pollux by the hand.
Now endless evening, like a painted band,
Starts moving, moving past us, and we seize,
Soft-reaching, all that momently can please.
There is an hour for singing, when the book
Lies open, and a rolling eye may look
For prompting at the words of Nelly Gray,
Darby and Joan, The Miller, Old Dog Tray;
Malbrouck that went to war, and Hoosen Johnny;
Or over the ocean, over the sea my bonnie.
The dominoes that once amused us well
Lie in their box and envy bagatelle,
Whose twenty balls, thrust up the tilted board,
Pause and return—click, click—a thousand scored!
With game or song the clock goes round to eight:
Past time for two to sleep, whose laggard gait
We must not hope to hurry up the landing.
Each elder then knows where a book is standing,
Tall on the crowded table; and begins
What may go on until the darkness thins:
Page after page upturned against the light.
For so it was, on such a nipping night,
That Holmes, or Doctor Thorndyke, heard the bell
And raced with lawless death to Camberwell;
Or Watson, in an alley with his master,
Felt the steel fingers as a crutch came faster:
Tapping, tapping, tapping, till the court
Blazed with a sudden pistol's blind report.
This is the hour, and this the placeless room

For smooth concocted tales of lust and doom;
This the remote, the sanctuary year
When the safe soul must fabricate a fear.
Many a milder evening passes, too,
With Royal Casino, Rummy, and a few
Swift-changing hands of High-Low-Jack-and-the-Game.
But then three weeks ago the chessmen came;
Since when, no night so busy that it misses
The march of angry Queens, whose scalloped tresses,
Stiffly erected, fly to guard a King.
We are two novices, and rashly fling
Pawns, bishops, knights, and rooks into the fray;
Yet time and blood have taught us wiser play.
There was a gift at Christmas time of Tarot—
Untaught, but we can shuffle them and harrow
A loreless mind with him, the Hanging Man;
So all those numbered mysteries that plan
What future folds the player, and what past
Is carved upon the great Tower overcast,
So every wand and pentacle and sword
Lies curious, unfathomed, on the board.
We have been known, as never back in town,
To idle till the clock weights settled down,
And till the sound of ticking ceased unheard.
We have rejoiced some evenings at the word
Of neighbors driving over; when the names,
Smith, Prentice, Landeck, interrupted games
With something else of equal clear delight.
For there was talking now into the night,
With news of health, and trips away from home,
And how the kitchen beer went all to foam.
Gossip of Hautboy, Dibble, and Great Hill,
Gossip and jest and argument, until:
Goodbye, Smith, Landeck, Prentice; come again;
Good night. And so a day is ended then.
Each four and twenty hours, until we rise,
Go thus. And thus the holy winter flies.

. . . February flies, with little summers
Hidden in its beard: unlicensed mummers
Performing April antics for a day.
The sun from the horizon swings away;
The sky melts upward, and a windless hand
Scatters the seeds of warmth along the land.
They will not grow, for ice is underneath,
And every creature tastes it. But a wreath
Lies thrown by playful chance upon the smiling
Meadows that a season is beguiling.
Today was so, but we were not deceived;
Though what the wolf-dog and the cats believed
There is no art of knowing. They pursued
Our every venturing step and found it good:
Down the crisp meadows to the aspen grove;
Over the highway, where a salesman drove
Dry wheels on dry macadam; then the neck
Of Harrison's pasture to the Hollenbeck.
We stood, the seven walkers, on a stone
And watched the river, waveless and alone,
Go slipping, slipping under, gravelly clear.
Snippy, a mile from nowhere, crouched to peer
At nothing in the sand; then bolder sat.
Three weeks, we said, and she would be a cat
With fearsome crying kittens of her own.
Ten months with us, no more, and nearly grown!
So Snappy, arriving plump and solemn there,
Good-natured sat, the guardian of the pair.
There was a barn foundation to explore,
Ancient of fields beyond. The rotting floor
Forewarned us, and we did not enter in;
But strolled, and where tall timothy had been
Lay half an hour on stubble under the sun;
While Sam, excited by a scent, must run
Low-whining up the fences; till a voice
Recalled him, and we made the hapless choice

Of eastward marshy meadows for return.
The hummocks mired us, but a cat could learn
The causeway's secret truth; and what we lost
Came back to us at home with tea and toast.

. . . Since yesterday a hundred years have gone.
The fore-and-after season, living on,
Rouses itself and finds its bitter breath.
This wind holds on to winter as to death.
There is no end, we say, and sauntering out,
Northwestward lean till we are whirled about,
Mute neck and shoulders stinging with the snow;
Or on this Sunday morning think to go,
Foot-heavy, where the giant maples spread
Their smooth enormous branches, long since dead.
Still in this waste of wind they do not fall;
But stiffen, like old serpents sent to crawl
On dense, on layered air; until the charm
Is lifted, and descending out of harm,
They lie leaf-covered, rigid in decay
Until the last small worm has turned away.
Here in the woodland clearings they patrol,
The wind drives steadily upon its goal.
But yonder where the hemlocks lace together
There is a sudden calm, a death of weather.
The shade is black, as once in late July
When here we walked escaping yellow sky.
The shade is black and even, and the snow
Comes filtered to the open cones below:
Slowly, slowly, slowly; strange the hush,
Here in this darkened desert of the thrush.
No hermits now; yet bands of chicadees
Tread fearless of us, chirping in the trees.
The ferns of June are withered on the rocks
Midway the icy stream that bends and locks
This needled promontory where we stand.

Oh, happy time! when nothing makes demand;
When all the earth, surrendering its strength,
Regains a taller potency at length;
Sleeps on in purest might of nothing done
Till summer heaves on high the exacting sun.

. . . Ice everywhere, a comic inch of it.
Four veteran walkers of a sudden sit
Wide-sprawling; but the cat that went so sure
Waits in the shed, distrustful and demure.
On this one day the dark mare, left inside,
Stands munching while the startled ponies slide—
Their path a river, and the river frozen—
Until a barn's captivity is chosen.
Ice everywhere; but over Goshen way
Ice on the mountains: murderous display.
Down the wild road to where the lanes were dry
We crept on crunching chains; then letting fly,
Passed houses till we gained the known plateau.
Yet now no more familiar, for the glow
Of crystals, like an ocean, blinded eyes
Untutored in the way a forest dies:
Slim birch and maple, sycamore and larch

Bent low before the mysteries of March;
Bent glassy-low, or splintered to a heap
Of glittering fragments that the sunrays sweep—
The sun, ironic, heartless, come to glance
At death and beauty shivering in a dance.

. . . I have been absent through the ending days
Of March beyond the mountains, where the ways
Of all the world drive onward as before.
I have been absent from the windy door;
Have gazed on travel-mornings out of flying
Windows at a distant winter dying.
But not our own, I said; and still believe
There will be news at home of its reprieve.
Nothing of that can change. And yet the doubt
Creeps into me as I look homesick out
On farms that are reminding me of one
Not distant now, beneath the selfsame sun.
A further valley, and a further range,
And I shall see if anything be strange.
Another dozen stations, and the three
I have been absent from will run to me,
And tell me if they know. At which the tears
Come premature, and stillness stops my ears.

. . . That very Wednesday, going to Great Hill,
The ruts all melted and the road was swill;
The hub caps foundered, and a number plate
Rose out of mire to recognize the spate.
All underground was overflowing for us,
Helpless until a wakened workhorse bore us,
Backward, absurd, to dry macadam land.
So April, with a wild unwelcome hand,
Showers proof upon us here of winter gone.
Our visitors on Friday night are wan:
Town-tired, and do not know it till we tell them.
The stripling cats, until we thought to bell them,
Havocked among the juncos, dropped to feed
On what the lawn still held of husk or seed.
A hundred misty bellies and blue backs
Move unmolested northward, leaving tracks
On certain darker mornings when a flurry
Satins the ground—not deep enough to worry
Those busy bills that, helped by hopping feet,
Find out the fruit of barberries and eat.
The apple barrels, picked over, have revealed
How many Baldwins never will be peeled;
The fungus spreads, and spots of deathly white
Show where the teeth of time have been to bite.
The wolf-dog has abandoned us by day;
He is in love across the scented way.
Nothing can keep him when the wind arrives;
He chews his chain, or alternately strives
Till the round collar slips and he goes running.
The ponies' noses have as old a cunning.
There is no forage yet, but they can smell
Green tropics creeping hither, and will fell
Each night a length of fence for dumb escape;
Then stumble back at breakfast time and gape,
Wit-withered, at the breach they cannot solve.
So, as the weeks implacably revolve

128

Of early, windy April, come the sprays
Of wood viburnum in the pathless ways
Where rocks and bent witch-hazel boughs declare
Once more their truce, awakening to air.
So, as the world turned sunward, Snippy died.
In the dim middle of a night she cried,
Desperate upon the steps; and lived a day.
But we have laid her slenderly away.
Her young within her she was not to bear;
So Snappy sits disconsolately there,
Under the branching crab tree; faced about,
Fixed on the clods, as if to stare her out.

. . . Spring is not yet; though how can this be long:
This crush of silence, this untimely-wrong,
Wide, cruel weight of whiteness, wing-descended
Even as we declared the winter ended?
Last night it happened. Everything, unwarned,
Suffered the soundless swoop of him the Horned,
The Universal Owl, whose ruthless plumes
Settled like death, distributing our dooms;
No feather heavy, but the sum of all
Seemed ultimate: earth's sepulchre and pall.
Not a flake settled on the flimsiest twig
But stayed; until this morning all were big
With monstrous moveless worms, that in the sun
Drip swiftly; but the evil has been done.
How fair it was last evening, when our lamp
Shone out on fleecy lilacs; yet the damp,
The clammy hand of this last dying snow—
How terrible to touch, and inly know:
This is the breaking end. So now at noon,
Divided, we behold the orchard strewn
With murdered buds and down-demolished branches.
So, by the graveyard, death upon its haunches
Sits in the form of great-grandfather-pine's

Chiefest of giant limbs, whose blackened lines
Trace there a new design of death across
Bare stones for whom no novelty of loss,
No morning news of woe can tell them more
Than that another winter shuts the door.
Divided thus—admiring, yet appalled—
We watch the season, poor, unfuneralled,
Pass with no mourners on; and recognize
What most we loved here impotent to rise.
If any sight could soften us to spring,
It is this melted, this emaciate thing.

. . . So April's plumefall was the last one, leaving
Nothing behind save midmonth warmth, and heaving
Roots, rain-drenched on many a sodden day.
Now even the rain is gone, that kept us grey;
Even the rain, preserving darkness too.
After the flood dry weather, hot and blue,
Washed every stain of winter off, and brightly
Gave us this world, so changeable and sightly:
Grass upon the mountains; smokeless-green
May fire that will not languish till the lean,
Brown, bitten earth, monotonous with stone,
Hides under hotness, leafy and alone;
Shade everywhere—as here beneath the crab,
Where Snippy lies, and rumors of Queen Mab
Bring bees to set the blossoms in a roar
While marvelling children pace the petalled floor;
Shade then for her, the borrowed Tabby, lying
With three new kittens, curious and crying:
The summer's offspring, not to be confused
With those somehow more brave that March misused.
Now the sleek mare is shod again, and trots
Each day beneath her mistress, over lots
Green-rising, or along a sandy road:
Each of them glad, the bearer and the load;

130

But I that walk to meet them down the lawn
Remember lazy mornings lost and gone:
Remember the cold, remember the lantern, hanging
There by her nose at night, and blizzards banging
Somewhere a shabby door; and my decision
Goes to the old, the February vision.
How old it is now, only a rake and spade;
Only a wolf-dog, panting in the shade;
Only a coatless, an oblivious pair
Of boys for whom all days to come are fair;
Only her warm hand, patting down the seed
Where sunlight lingers and the frost is freed;
Only the hay-land, live again with snakes;
Only these things can say what memory aches—
Oh, vainly—to recapture; only such
Can tell of the holy time our blood will touch—
Oh, never again, and never; only June,
That sings of something over deathly soon.
Already the mind's forgetfulness has blended
Music with music; and the months are ended.